3/2

CHICK FLICKS

CHICK FLICKS

A Movie Lover's Guide to the Movies Women Love

JAMI BERNARD

A Citadel Press Book
Published by Carol Publishing Group

A Citadel Press Book
Published by Carol Publishing Group
Citadel Press is a registered trademark of Carol Communications, Inc.
Editorial, sales and distribution, rights and permissions inquiries should be addressed to Carol Publishing Group, 120 Enterprise Avenue, Secaucus, N.J. 07094.
In Canada: Canadian Manda Group, One Atlantic Avenue, Suite 105, Toronto, Ontario M6K 3E7

Carol Publishing Books may be purchased in bulk at special discounts for sales promotion, fund-raising, or educational purposes. Special editions can be created to specifications. For details, contact: Special Sales Department, Carol Publishing Group, 120 Enterprise Avenue, Secaucus, N.J. 07094.

Manufactured in the United States of America
10 9 8 7 6 5 4 3 2 1

Library of Congress Cataloging-in-Publication Data

Bernard, Jami.
    Chick flicks : a movie lover's guide to the movies women love / Jami Bernard.
        p.   cm.
    "A Citadel Press book."
    ISBN 0-8065-1836-7 (pbk.)
    1. Motion pictures for women—Catalogs. I. Title.
PN 1995.9.W6B39   1996
016.79143′75′082—dc20   96–36123
                                                     CIP

This book is dedicated to the women in my life who are always happy to cry at a good chick flick, even a bad one: Amanda, Diane B., Diane S., Dorrie, Gloria, JoAnne, and Meg.

Contents

Preface

As a film critic, I can sit through anything. But what I can sit through and what I really love are very different. Me, I'd take a good Chick Flick over almost anything else.

Men, on the other hand, would rather choke on a beer pretzel than go to a Chick Flick. Men don't want to sit through romances, tearjerkers, or relationship movies. They have little interest in stories about women, families, or the heartbreaks and triumphs of everyday living. Chick Flicks are perceived—as a Neanderthal ex-boyfriend of mine used to say—as "yet another sensitive story of a young girl's coming of age."

There are film critics who will tell you that there is no such thing as a Chick Flick—that is, a movie that appeals mostly to women. These critics insist that movies have such universal appeal that they transcend culture, class, and gender.

Well, I'm a film critic, and I'm telling you to wake up and smell the Junior Mints.

You have only to step into the various compartments of a multiplex to see that in the real world movies usually fall on one or the other side of the gender slope. There are Chick Flicks, and there are Guy Movies. Rarely do the twain meet.

That doesn't mean that men and women can't enjoy each other's films. As I explain later in this book, a Guy Movie, like the Schwarzenegger actionfest *True Lies*, can be enjoyed by women on an entirely different level. That makes sense, because movies with half a brain in them were *meant* to be enjoyed on several levels at once. That is why dialogue has subtext, the meaning behind the meaning.

In 1991 the romantic comedy *Sleepless in Seattle* attempted to explain the phenomenon of the Chick Flick. The difference between the sexes, the movie argued, can be seen in the way in which men and women respond to the 1957 romantic chestnut *An Affair to Remember*. In that movie, when Cary Grant realizes that Deborah Kerr has not wanted to burden him with her paraplegia, women cry—always a good sign in a Chick Flick. *Sleepless in Seattle* goes on to say, only half jokingly, that a male audience can attain the same moist pleasure only from watching the wartime suicide mission in *The Dirty Dozen*.

Sleepless in Seattle was not infallible in its reasoning. I've always adored *The Dirty Dozen* and found *An Affair to Remember* too sodden. But that's just me.

And that's something to keep in mind; movies provide very subjective experiences. I can't promise that each of the seventy-five Chick Flicks in this book will resonate with each female or turn off every man. Maybe you're a woman who has a secret yen for *Porky's*. (There is help available for you.) Maybe you're a guy reading this book for some insight into women and you're wondering what all the fuss is, since you loved *Thelma & Louise*, too.

So what is a Chick Flick, anyway? Is it a sappy romance, a maudlin tearjerker?

It used to be. In the 1940s everyone acknowledged the existence of the Chick Flick. Back then they called it a "woman's picture," and heterosexual men wouldn't go near one. They were plush, lush melodramas featuring the era's biggest female stars: Rosalind Russell, Claudette Colbert, Irene Dunne, Bette Davis, Joan Crawford, Norma Shearer, Jean Arthur, Barbara Stanwyck.

These movies were designed to appeal to a female audience "of a certain age"—mothers, grandmothers, working women, maiden aunts—who shared the same moral viewpoint and could empathize with the trials and tribulations of these not-larger-than-life characters.

In today's parlance, a Chick Flick is much more than a melodrama. It is any movie that makes a special connection with a female audience. It can be defined by the qualities it has that usually attract women—female stars, familial situations, cute guys, emotional catharsis. Or it can be defined in reverse, by just how far afield it is from a typical Guy Movie.

Compare *The Piano* with, say, *Crimson Tide*. One features a tantalizingly slow romantic buildup between two people in nineteenth-century New Zealand who struggle to communicate their innermost passions. The other is about jockeying for who gets to push the control buttons on a nuclear sub. Which would you say is the Chick Flick? The Guy Movie?

The humorist Dave Barry once pointed out that "as a rule, guys don't care for movies with a lot of dialogue. Guys become bored if a movie character speaks more than two consecutive sentences without some kind of important plot development: punching, explosions, aliens, car chases, or Sharon Stone recrossing her legs."

Barry went on to imagine *The Bridges of Madison County* (a Chick Flick) as it could have been made for a male audience. In the actual movie, Iowa housewife Meryl Streep has a weekend fling with Clint Eastwood, who remains the secret love of her life, even beyond the grave. In Barry's imaginary version, Streep starts the movie by getting naked to look at herself in the mirror. In scene 2 she is working in the cornfield in a thong bikini when Keanu Reeves pulls up. Barry's scenario continues, with more sex and other possible sexual partners.

It's not that women don't want sex in their movies. It's just that they want sex they can relate to. As my Aunt Sandy likes to say, "Women give sex to get love, and men say they love in order to get sex." In a good Chick Flick there is plenty of sex for women, *and* they are truly loved; the universe is complete.

There are many factors that make a Chick Flick so appealing to women. One could be as simple as a strong female cast; another, subject matter with which they can identify. The movie may have an adorable male lead—the "Hunks" section easily could have been expanded to fill an entire book of its own. Just because I've left out Brad, Mel, Liam, and Bruce doesn't mean they weren't on my mind. (Lord knows, they were.) But there is more to a Chick Flick than just a hunky guy, and my goal was to give a range of examples from different eras in each category of Chick Flick, from a legendary catfight like *All About Eve* to the familiar pangs of the schoolgirl crush in *To Sir With Love* to the adorable mall girl of *Clueless*.

A movie doesn't have to be soft and gentle to be a Chick Flick. The high-tech action thrillers *True Lies* and *La Femme Nikita* are included here. A movie doesn't have to be nice to women to appeal to them: *9 1/2 Weeks* features Kim Basinger in a notoriously sadomasochistic relationship, and Glenn Ford admits in *Gilda* that he regards Rita Hayworth as no better than a sack of laundry.

Sometimes the real reason women relate to a movie is not very flattering. What I report in this book may offend or even scandalize. Truth can do that. You may never look at some of these movies in the same way again after they've been deconstructed for the feminine subconscious. The lusty musical *Seven Brides for Seven Brothers* is a rape fantasy, after all. And the most romantic scene ever filmed—Rhett carrying Scarlett up the staircase—is another rape.

Sure, I've included traditional romances like *Sabrina* and old weepies like *Waterloo Bridge*. But I've also popped the lid off the real reason women are drawn to the sadomasochism of *Carmen Jones* and the repressed guilt of *The Bad Seed*. *National Velvet* is not just a story of a girl and her horse; it also concerns the secret passing of a torch from mother to daughter. *Picnic*, which we usually watch for William Holden's bare chest, is also about a girl and her mother—in this case, a girl struggling to free herself from her mom's choke hold. Ditto *Frances*.

The Professional, which seemingly concerns a recalcitrant hit man, is really about a father making the ultimate sacrifice for his daughter. *Jane Eyre* is about getting rid of mommy to marry daddy—the Electra complex. So is *Gaslight*, a more guilt-ridden movie. So is *Working Girl*—and you thought it was about Melanie Griffith landing a better job.

Women only want what men want—movies that are well-made, interesting, and appeal to their different intellectual and emotional needs. They want to be thrilled, calmed, and entertained.

While it's true that most movies are made primarily by men for a male audience—particularly a young, car-crash-loving male audience—don't be fooled into thinking that there's nothing out there for women. I pared down a list of hundreds to arrive at the seventy-five Chick Flicks in this book.

It was excruciating to decide what would stay and what would go. No book on Chick Flicks could do without *Gone With the Wind*, yet it pained me to leave out the 1931 German film *Maedchen in Uniform*, scandalous in its time for portraying a lesbian relationship in a girls' boarding school.

After much agonizing, I left out *The Way We Were*, but just had to make room for the Chinese film *Raise the Red Lantern*, which has so much to say about women and powerlessness.

The result is an eclectic mix of Chick Flicks for every taste, from every era.

Needless to say, there are few car chases.

TEARJERKERS

To many women, a good cry is worth the price of admission. The tears are cathartic and are usually a mix of happiness and frustration, which is why the best tearjerkers are ones in which the heroine comes just this close to heaven before fate intervenes or must nobly renounce her happiness for the good of others. In *The Bridges of Madison County*, Meryl Streep abandons love for the sake of her family; in *Intermezzo*, Ingrid Bergman does so for the sake of his. In *Casablanca*, Bergman sacrifices her heart to the war effort. Bette Davis had such a damaging upbringing in *Now, Voyager* that sharing cigarettes with Paul Henreid is the best she can manage. And, wouldn't you know it, just when Vivien Leigh realizes it's Clark Gable she's loved all along, he's out the door. Sniffle.

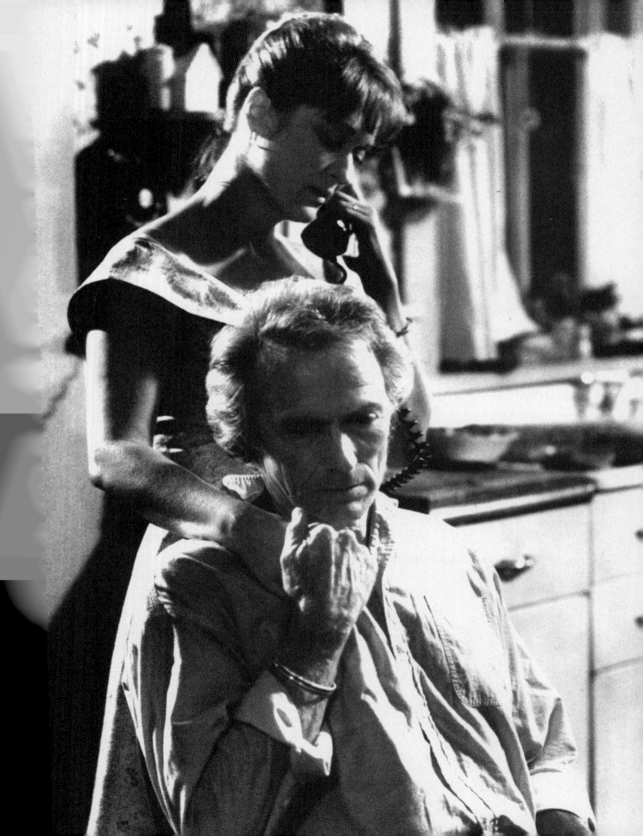

The Bridges of Madison County
1995

The path not taken fills women with equal measures of anxiety and longing. Would life have been better with the one that got away? *The Bridges of Madison County*, about a weekend fling that allows an ordinary housewife to experience the best of both worlds, answers that nagging question.

The late humorist Erma Bombeck thought the most thrilling thing about *The Bridges of Madison County* was that Francesca Johnson's husband would take the kids off her hands for four whole days to a state fair. To any housewife, that alone would be a godsend. Francesca (Meryl Streep) gets more joy than that out of the weekend; she has her first and only extramarital fling. As in *Brief Encounter*, it's enough to keep her chugging along in an otherwise boring marriage the rest of her days.

Robert James Waller's sentimental novel crept like a fungus across America until seemingly every woman who'd ever had a dull day was sobbing over it. Francesca is a perfect heroine for the masses because she is so unlike what you'd expect in a torrid romance: she's a middle-aged Italian war bride who has spent her adult life in a bland Iowa existence, raising children and tending to farm chores and her slow-pulse husband. There isn't much money, and there's even less excitement. When asked to describe her mate, she ponders, then comes up with: "He's very clean."

She doesn't dislike her life; it's just that it isn't quite what she had in mind as a girl. The everydayness of life can wear a person down.

Within moments of her weekend respite from hubby and kids, weather-beaten *National Geographic* photographer Robert Kincaid (Clint Eastwood) pulls up looking for the famous local covered bridges.

Housewife Meryl Streep makes her first contact with itinerant photographer Clint Eastwood in *The Bridges of Madison County*, a movie that explores the path not taken.

3

Francesca puts down her yard work and shows him the way; what the heck. Their unlikely affair has a slow, awkward beginning, mostly consisting of their sitting around Francesca's kitchen talking about what they expected of life versus what they got.

There is a simple moment when Francesca is on the phone with a neighbor while Robert is sitting on a kitchen chair. Francesca idly places her hand on Robert's shoulder, a very ordinary, yet personal, gesture, and he places his hand over hers. Unlike the purple passion of the novel, the movie is excitingly spare of feeling, allowing small tingles to accumulate—like the sensuality Francesca feels when she bathes in a tub so recently occupied by this strange new man.

And what could be more exciting to a homemaker than a lover who helps with the dishes?

Bridges would wholly be a Chick Flick if it were not for a framing device that acts as a Greek chorus for the skeptical. The four-day fling is told in flashback after Francesca's death, when her two grown children find her diaries and love letters and piece together Mom's secret life. "Now I find out that between bake sales my mother was Anaïs Nin!" exclaims the daughter. The grown son expresses dismay, as if echoing the men in the audience who have to be dragged into the mushy love story like horses crossing a rain-swollen stream. Whenever the romance gets too intense, the grown son reappears to give the men out there a breather, while the female audience impatiently await the resumption of the four-day fling. (Women realize that Francesca is planning to go all the way when she spends household money to buy a new dress.)

Francesca almost takes wing with Robert, but in a last-minute, rainy farewell, she renounces him for the good of all. In this way, Francesca gets to retain her housewifely halo, seeing her husband through to the end, as she vowed on their wedding day. But she also gets to have tasted the grand passion that every woman dreams of—the one man who was a soul mate, who will never forget you or recover from the loss of you, the marital safety valve that is always lurking in the background.

Naturally, the audience wants Francesca to run off and live large with the photographer. But she is wiser and knows that any relationship that has a chance to achieve that blessed everydayness will suffer from it as well. *The shorter the fling, the greater the passion*. Four days seems about right.

Casablanca

1942

Since the release of *Casablanca* in 1942, everybody has gone to Rick's—
and more than a few times.

They know all about Humphrey Bogart bitterly pining away in his
North African cafe for Ingrid Bergman, who left him a cold farewell note
as his train chugged out of Paris. They know why she left him—that little
matter of Paul Henreid redux. They know that even though this is considered a classic example of the Oedipal drama, women stick to this movie
like glue, or like travelers in Casablanca without letters of transit.

So let's leave aside the letters of transit for a moment; they're the
biggest maguffin of them all. ("They cannot be rescinded or even ques-
tioned"—oh, sure.) Instead, we'll concentrate on Rick and Ilsa—Bogart
and Bergman—having wartime sex.

What—you don't remember Rick and Ilsa having sex in the most
famous and romantic love triangle in cinematic history? They have sex
at least twice in the movie; you just have to watch for it carefully.

They first have sex in Paris. They'll *always* have Paris. The Germans
wore gray; Ilsa wore blue. Surely you remember *that*.

Before she stood up Rick at the train station, Ilsa was in his apartment with him. They were toasting each other cozily with champagne.
What are they celebrating? Ilsa is wearing what appears to be a dressing
gown; it must be morning—or worse, afternoon!—and they have just
climbed out of bed. Either that or Rick was delivering room service as a
career before becoming the proprietor of Rick's Cafe Americain.

"Who are you really? And what were you before? What did you do,
and what did you think? Huh?" asks Rick in what can only be described
as postcoital babbling.

"We said 'no questions,' " reminds Ilsa in what can only be described
as precoital precaution.

Bogart and Bergman have more than Paris. They have at least two sexual escapades during the course of *Casablanca* before parting on the tarmac.

Now we fast-forward what feels like years to the corrupt city of Casablanca, although in the time frame of the movie it's only about six months later. Despite Rick's hardness and claims of neutrality, he's just a big softie, helping young couples get exit visas and wheeling and dealing with Captain Renault (Claude Rains), the police prefect who is *shocked* to find gambling at Rick's as he pockets his winnings.

Of all the gin joints in all the towns all over the world, Ilsa walks into Rick's. Sure, she could have gone to the Blue Parrot across the way, but as the original working title of the movie made clear, Everybody Goes to Rick's.

Rick is still raw from grieving, which is why we can forgive the way he brutishly ignores his current girlfriend, sending her home in a taxi when she drinks too much. We already know he's a decent guy because the first time we see him in the movie he is playing chess against himself, his finger on the white pawn.

Still, Rick is not one to forgive easily. He sits at Ilsa's table and snipes away at her, raising the eyebrows of the man who brought her there, resistance fighter Victor Laszlo (Paul Henreid). If Laszlo can't guess that

Ilsa had an affair with Rick in Paris, then he's the only one in town who doesn't know. When Sydney Greenstreet, owner of the rival nightclub the Blue Parrot, tells Henreid that he thinks Rick has the letters of transit, Greenstreet looks pointedly at Ilsa, and she blushes.

And what an affair it was. Rick is still so bitter over the rejection, he takes to the bottle later that night, getting maudlin while Sam the piano man takes him on a five-finger walk down memory lane. "You know what I want to hear," Rick berates his pianist. "You played it for her; you can play it for me. If she can stand it, I can. Play it!"

As time goes by, Ilsa shows up. Rick insults her and implies she's a whore. ("Or aren't you the kind who tells?")

The next day, he tries to apologize to her at an outdoor bazaar, but she ain't buying. He learns that Ilsa is—and was—married to Laszlo.

Nevertheless, that very night, she appears at Rick's apartment over the cafe with a gun held unsteadily in her hand. What would she do for those letters of transit? Well, what *wouldn't* she do! She tries to appeal to Rick's sense of patriotism, to the memory of their love, to whatever might sway him. She says she'd do anything to get those papers. But she loves him too much to shoot him, and after this becomes clear, they have sex again—and this time there's no excuse that maybe Victor is dead in a concentration camp somewhere.

"The day you left Paris, if you knew what I went through!" she cries. "If you knew how much I loved you, how much I still love you!"

They fall into each other's arms, kissing passionately. Cut to Rick by the open window smoking a cigarette. And we know what *that* means.

The psychology of the multi-Oscar-winning movie says it's about Rick resolving his Oedipal complex, learning to leave Mommy to Daddy and move on with his life. As far as women are concerned, it's about regaining the lost love of your live—and enjoying it, too. Although no one wants Ilsa to stay with that dreary resistance fighter, at least she's had her fun and managed to stay respectable. For Ilsa, and the women who identify with her, this is the end of a beautiful friendship.

Gone With the Wind
1939

When Rhett sweeps Scarlett up that grand staircase in *Gone With the Wind*, it is arguably the most romantic moment in film history.

And that's a rape scene.

Gone With the Wind is considered the epitome of romance. The selfish, flirtatious, iron-willed Scarlett needs a man's man like Rhett to tame her, someone who can stand his ground and who can decide, on Scarlett's behalf, that she "should be kissed, and kissed often, by someone who knows how"—*kissing* being one of those old-movie euphemisms open to interpretation. Apparently, Rhett is the only such man in the Civil War–torn South. Audiences go wild with sobbing when he walks out on Scarlett at the end.

Let's assume we are all familiar with the plot; nay, with every frame of the movie. Let's turn our attention instead to Rhett Butler and see what kind of character is the most desired man in cinema history. What follows will deconstruct Rhett into a man you might despise, the point being that such a man is the kind women are conditioned to long for. It matters not that in real life such a man would break your heart, and not prettily.

Rhett is a gambler. We smile indulgently when we see him happily "losing" to his Union captors in endless games of jailhouse poker. By so doing, he gets special privileges, like conjugal visits in his cell from the prostitute Belle Watley. Scarlett makes a dress out of her drapes—a concept no woman has ever quite gotten over the wonderment of—and visits Rhett in jail to coax rent money out of him to save the plantation Tara. All this begs the question of whether Rhett's gambling is an adorable, manly activity or an addiction that could bankrupt Scarlett down the road.

Rhett lives by a double standard. He's tickled to see Scarlett weathering the war so well until he sees that her hands are rough and calloused from eking out an existence. Instead of having compassion for what this proud

Dreamboat Clark Gable is perfect for Vivien Leigh, even though he gambles, wenches, drinks too much, and rapes her in *Gone With the Wind*.

woman had to do to survive—goodness, she threw up from eating tubers just as the sun was setting and the theme song was swelling!—he turns her away because she's no longer the fine, baby-soft lady he once knew.

Rhett is unreliable. First he declines to join his brethren, the Confederates, because he believes the North will win, anyway. He makes his wartime living as a mercenary, a paid blockade runner. Later, he flip-flops. After getting Scarlett and ailing new mother Melanie out of blazing Atlanta, he runs off to join the soldiers he's snubbed, and we do mean he runs off. Despite scattered musket fire, he doesn't bother to see the two ladies to their door. He just leaves them stranded on the road after giving Scarlett his calling card, a dazzling kiss.

Rhett is sexually unfaithful. Belle Watley could never trade up after Rhett put so much mileage on her. You could argue that Scarlett drives Rhett to the whorehouse because she won't sleep with him after their first baby for fear pregnancy will ruin her figure. Strictly speaking, he's still breaking his marriage vows, and he's doing it with prostitutes, from whom he could be tracking nasty diseases. Scarlett only lusts for Ashley in her heart and never actually breaks her vows.

Rhett is a good-time Charlie and a drunk. Mostly he's a pleasant drunk, which only adds to his appeal. But when he gets really into his cups, he's capable of rape. Although Scarlett clearly liked it and Rhett apologizes the next morning for having been swept away by her "charms" (blame the victim!), it was still a rape. His response is to abandon her (and take her child away, too).

Rhett has a mother-whore complex. Although he appreciates Scarlett's fiery temperament and tricky ways, once they're married, he infantilizes her. He prefers her to sit around being silly and pretty and receptive to gifts instead of having her use her drive and business savvy either for profit or personal gratification. When he thinks she's cheating on him with the milquetoast Ashley Wilkes, Rhett forces her to dress in red like a harlot and go to Melanie's birthday party alone as punishment.

If Rhett Butler were to catch your eye today, here's what you might get: an occasionally sadistic boozer who cheats on you, hangs out at OTB, won't "let" you work because his ego demands that he be the breadwinner, and controls your life even down to what you should wear and how revealing it can be. Since he is repelled by neediness, he might turn a cold shoulder when you are most vulnerable. He'd be a man eligible for any number of twelve-step programs but won't join because they'd cramp his style. He might take your child away from you as a punishment. After he carried you up the stairs to rape you, you wouldn't smile dreamily like Scarlett. Instead, you'd spend the night at a shelter for abused women, worrying that the court order that keeps him at a safe distance won't necessarily stop him from stalking you in a drunken fit; after all, he has been obsessed and flirting with you through your previous marriages.

Now let's look at Rhett from the other side of the camera.

While the nationwide search for an actress to play Scarlett was unprecedented then and now, the role of Rhett was always thought of as

Gable's. The trouble was, he didn't want it, not "for money, marbles, or chalk," as he told producer David O. Selznick.

The author of the bestselling *Gone With the Wind* novel, Margaret Mitchell, was horrified by the possibility of Gable in the role, claiming that the South had rallied behind the choice of Basil Rathbone. When Gable's wife, Carole Lombard, gave him the book to read, Gable said his "reaction to Rhett was immediate and enthusiastic—what a part for Ronald Colman."

Vivien Leigh, hired at long last during the filming of the burning of Atlanta, didn't enjoy playing opposite Gable. She thought he was unprofessional (he indulged in constant breaks), and his dentures stank during their kissing scenes; no wonder she seemed to swoon from his caresses.

Knowing any or all of this doesn't make a difference to the legions of women who adore Rhett. When he walks out, not giving a damn, every female's engines are revved to win him back. It's a point of pride. He may be a low-down, dirty skunk—but he's *my* low-down, dirty skunk!

Intermezzo
1939

In *Intermezzo*, Stravinsky's *Rite of Spring* is not only a musical theme; it's also a metaphor for Leslie Howard's midlife crisis. "That spring you spoke of," his wife gently tells him, "that sort of happiness comes only once in life."

But for concert violinist Holger Brandt (Howard), it comes twice in life, when his children's comely piano teacher reawakens his senses.

Holger doesn't notice Anita Hoffman (Ingrid Bergman) until she sits at the keyboard. Then she plays so passionately, her face as radiant as cinematographer Gregg Toland can make it—which isn't hard to do when it's the young Bergman—that Holger picks up his violin and they start a duet that, in the larger sense, will eventually ruin his marriage. She pounds out the chords on the piano while his delicate eyelids flutter.

"I'm listening to something," says Holger, staring off into the distance during his first romantic walk with Anita.

"Spring, perhaps?" she says.

"Yes, perhaps."

Holger's extramarital affair puts the spring back in his step. Before long, he has left his wife and children, and he and Anita are touring the concert halls of Europe. She accompanies him on the piano, and they finish their performances with the theme song of their love, "Intermezzo," a haunting, yearning piece that triggers Pavlovian tears in any woman who has ever seen the movie.

"*Mon amour dure après la mort*" (My love endures after death) reads a tombstone on the French Riviera, where the couple is enjoying a romantic idyll. "That was written for us and for everyone on earth who feel as we do now," says Holger as hearts crack open like walnuts in the theater.

As if the haunting music weren't enough to remind us, this love affair is doomed. That their eternal devotion is carved on a tombstone is just

Music student Ingrid Bergman and married violinist Leslie Howard are making beautiful music together, but notice the barren tree behind them— a sign that their love is only an *Intermezzo* in their lives.

one nail in the coffin. "I wonder if anyone has ever built happiness on the unhappiness of others," Anita's aged tutor tells her when he visits, stirring restless pangs of guilt.

Despite the audience's emotional investment in the illicit affair, Anita leaves Holger, realizing that it's for the best: "I have been an intermezzo in his life."

It's not as if Anita will be ruined by the breakup; there is, after all, the Jenny Lind music scholarship awaiting her in Paris. But the morally superior ending of Holger's life back in Sweden with lackluster wife Edna Best doesn't seem very enticing. Even the manipulative trick of having the adorable daughter hit by a car as she runs to greet the prodigal father isn't enough to quell the audience's regrets. "We're all human, tragically human," Holger tells his resentful son, wiping away his indiscretion with a weak *mea culpa*.

Could there have been another ending, the one the audience craves, in which Holger and Anita stay happily together in the south of France?

Not likely. For one thing, the movie has nowhere interesting to go once the lovers are out of hiding; no love affair is in spring bloom forever. Furthermore, the same public that cries out of pity for Bergman's character in *Intermezzo* was outraged by the actress's similar behavior in real life. This was Bergman's first American film, but even after she was a bona fide star, she was drummed out of the country for her later affair with married director Roberto Rossellini. Audiences have their own midlife crises with which to deal, which is why affairs on celluloid bring tears of catharsis and in real life bring lawsuits.

Now, Voyager

1942

Why ask for the moon when you have the stars?

That's a question many a mistress has asked herself over the course of an affair with a married man. Sometimes they phrase it to themselves the way Bette Davis does at the tear-stained finale of *Now, Voyager*—as in *"Don't* ask for the moon," etc. A woman like Charlotte Vale never had much faith in herself, anyway, and certainly never expected the day to come when Paul Henreid would be lighting two cigarettes at once, one for him and one for her.

Another woman, one with slightly more wisdom of the world than a brief stopover in Rio, might well wonder whether she's shortchanging herself with all those stars and no moonlight to come home to. But that's not Charlotte.

The love between former sad sack Charlotte Vale and permanently married Jerry Durrance brings tears to the viewer for two reasons. First, because it is stuck forever in a limbo of unattainability. Charlotte becomes a surrogate mother to Jerry's shy little girl, so that when the three are together, it's like playing house—all fun and none of the chores.

Another reason for the waterworks is because women understand just how far Charlotte had to come personally to get to that point with Jerry—how she had to break free of her mother's stranglehold on her self-esteem. That she can find any enjoyment in life after being made to feel so guilty about personal pleasure is a miracle.

It was Henreid's idea to light two cigarettes at once—such a suave, European gesture, immortalizing a scene that years later inspired the hit song "Bette Davis Eyes." Strange, then, that Davis had to fight to get Henreid as her costar; his first screen test was lousy, and she had to demand that he be tested again.

Why ask for the moon when your mother brought you up on crumbs? Bette Davis settles for the pure love of eternally married Paul Henreid in *Now, Voyager*.

Davis has referred to her character as "an undersexed Bostonian," but there's no telling how Charlotte would have turned out in a more encouraging environment. Charlotte meets Jerry on a cruise to South America. It is Charlotte's coming-out party, in a sense, because she has just recuperated in a sanitarium from a near breakdown. Her recovery isn't just emotional; it's cosmetic as well. She has lost twenty-five pounds, and once away from her sadistically disapproving mother (Gladys Cooper), she is able to let her hair down and take off those Coke-bottle glasses. Rarely has a famous actress allowed herself to look so terrible for dramatic purpose.

The sanitarium, run by Claude Rains, has worked its magic, if only to give Charlotte a break from Mom's sledgehammer disapproval for a few months. Physically she looks great, although she still doubts herself. "Every [family] has one, you know," she says when she describes herself as a maiden aunt, meaning a virgin, a spinster, a hanger-on.

"You haven't a very high opinion of yourself, have you?" asks Jerry kindly.

Like many a new girl on the block, Charlotte patterns herself after the first man who is kind to her. "Thank you for making me feel there were a few moments when I almost felt alive," she says, prostrating herself for crumbs of happiness. Even future marriage proposals from more available men will be turned down in favor of the shower of stars offered by Jerry.

"You fool," she tells herself. "Now you'll never have a home of your own, a man of your own, a child of your own."

Nevertheless, she gets what she wants in an awkward sort of way. She is faithful to Jerry all her life long (we suppose), and she takes on Jerry's child with a passion that would be alarming in real life. "This is Jerry's child in my arms," she tells herself, and thoughts of Glenn Close taking Michael Douglas's little girl to the amusement park in *Fatal Attraction* come to mind.

As for the house of her own, she practically runs it when she returns to care for her ailing mother and no longer lets anyone bully her. Then she actually kills her mother—at least in the Freudian sense—when Mom has a heart attack during an argument about Charlotte's love life. It's the ultimate guilt trip from beyond the grave.

At least Charlotte comes away with a home of her own, after all. Don't ask for the moon when you've got the kid, the house, and visitation rights with the man.

EMOTIONAL RESCUE

Women already know they aren't the frail damsels in distress of folklore. And that's just the problem. Most women are so busy working, taking care of the house and kids, and shouldering financial and emotional responsibilities that it would be a relief if, just once, a knight in shining armor would actually come riding up and lighten the load. In *The Bodyguard* and *Someone to Watch Over Me*, the rescue fantasy is quite literal—a man at your bedroom door whose sole purpose in life is to make you safe (and who can't help falling in love with you at the same time). In *The Piano*, Holly Hunter is trapped in her own body until she finds a man who understands her, even though she can't speak. In *Gaslight*, Ingrid Bergman is going to be driven crazy unless someone intervenes and takes her seriously. And in *Summertime*, Katharine Hepburn has one last chance in the autumn of life to find a man who can make her feel like a natural woman.

Despite the bad haircut, Kevin Costner in *The Bodyguard* is an appealing
embodiment of the strong, silent type, withholding his feelings only to protect
client Whitney Houston. How do we know he loves her? He watches her video
clips at night.

The Bodyguard

1992

As a famous performer who attracts dangerous fans, Rachel Marron genuinely needs what the rest of womankind only secretly wants: a man to watch over her body morning, noon, and night as if she were the most precious jewel.

Pop singer Whitney Houston made a successful acting debut as Rachel in *The Bodyguard*, a huge box-office hit, thanks largely to a female audience. If men love the idea that prostitutes would service them for free because they really love them, this is the female equivalent—that a man who is paid to care for you as a bodyguard would do it for love in any case.

In real life, Patty Hearst married her bodyguard. Princess Stephanie married hers. A handsome, strapping bodyguard whose only concern is your absolute protection is a more erotic, focused fantasy than the age-old policeman or fireman to the rescue.

Despite the awful crew cut he sports, Kevin Costner has never been sexier than as Frank Farmer, bodyguard extraordinaire. (The bad haircut is supposed to indicate that he is so intent on his work, he doesn't care about grooming.)

Anyway, he only *looks* square. "That's my disguise," he deadpans. True, he shuns liquor, jokes, and companionship, but he can slice the skin off a delicate peach and then hurl the same knife within a hair's breadth of a man's eye without breaking a sweat. After a prolonged and completely wordless punch-out with Rachel's former bodyguard, Frank coolly tells him: "I don't want to talk about this again." Now *that's* cool.

Frank is hired to protect megastar Rachel, a singer who has been nominated for an acting Oscar. She's been getting threatening notes and exploding dolls lately, and someone has been messing about in her bedsheets. She also has a solemn, intelligent son to think about.

At first, the glamorous Rachel doesn't want any bodyguard cramping her style, but she changes her mind when she realizes what a hunk he is. Although he seems to dislike her, he secretly watches her video clips at night out in the gardener's shed, and that's a real rush.

Frank is so on edge—it's a requirement of his job—that when he finally takes Rachel on a date to see *Yojimbo* and then to dinner, he cannot relax. A waiter drops a plate, and Frank is ready to assume the position.

The movie coils around this handsome couple's repressed sexual feelings for each other. Rachel torments Frank by having him guard her bedroom door while she's dallying with one of his fellow bodyguards, one who isn't nearly as proficient with a knife.

The role of Frank is Costner's sexiest, for *The Bodyguard* employs a tried-and-true romantic formula in which a man's remoteness is mistaken by the heroine for a lack of interest when, in fact, the audience cheerfully knows it is the opposite. This bodyguard simply cannot do his job when his eyes are clouded by love, and it's getting pretty cloudy lately.

Because Frank and Rachel are an interracial couple, the sex scene was trimmed considerably before the movie's release. That's a shame. The audience desperately wants to see them together, especially since Frank gives Rachel the heave-ho after just one night together. He can't mix business and pleasure; it would be against Rachel's interests. (He's breaking up with her for *her* sake, a line most women have surely heard but which never before this movie rang true.)

In a bit of outrageous dramatics, Frank takes the bullet for Rachel just as she is walking onstage to receive her Oscar. A man who will take a bullet for you? It's the most erotic present since gift certificates to Victoria's Secret.

Such a magnanimous gesture should tie these two kids together for life. But probably because of the interracial thing and the need to find an excuse for Houston's sob song of longing "I Will Always Love You," they part on the tarmac, *Casablanca* style. They'll always have the Dorothy Chandler Pavilion.

Gaslight
1944

Are those gaslights dimming, or is it just Ingrid Bergman going nuts?

She plays the emotionally delicate Paula Alquist in *Gaslight*. Paula isn't the first wife made to feel childish, clumsy, stupid, and forgetful by a condescending husband.

The difference here is that new hubby Gregory Anton (Charles Boyer) is deliberately trying to drive Paula mad, and he's doing a darn fine job. She's missing small items from her purse. She hears footsteps overhead in the locked attic. She's a virtual prisoner in the London house she inherited from her aunt, a famous singer whom Paula found murdered as a child.

The movie is a remake of a 1940 British version that M-G-M's Louis B. Mayer did his best to suppress. Bergman won her first Oscar for playing the gradually disintegrating Paula, and Joseph Cotten has never looked so warm and reassuring as he does coming to her rescue as a detective who senses something fishy at 9 Thornton Square.

Paula marries young, so you can hardly blame her for not noticing that her husband is more erratic than most men. He knows the history of each jewel in the Tower of London without the help of a guidebook, and he throws fits at the oddest times—for example, when Paula recovers a letter sent by a suitor to her aunt two days before the murder. Hmm. Could Gregory have something to hide?

"Are you afraid?" he asks her tenderly during their whirlwind courtship.

"Yes, a little."

"Of me?" he asks.

"No, never of you. Of happiness."

No need to fear, Paula. Happiness isn't coming your way anytime soon.

Ingrid Bergman, as yet unaware of Charles Boyer's nefarious intentions in *Gaslight*, embraces him with innocent affection. Soon he'll be driving her insane.

Paula's marriage is a living hell. She is accused of acting suspicious when she has every right to. Gregory chides her for her paranoia, which is entirely justified. Yes, the maid *does* hate her. (An eighteen-year-old Angela Lansbury plays the serving girl who offers special services to the man of the house.)

It's no wonder that women love *Gaslight*. Psychological abuse is a common weapon in the marital arsenal. Many wives have been so beaten down over the years by their husbands' disparaging comments that they doubt their judgment and abilities.

Paula would have snapped were it not for an eleventh-hour save by the intrepid detective, who thinks she's the most beautiful agoraphobe ever to crack up. "You're slowly and systematically being driven out of your mind," he reassures her.

This paves the way for Paula's moment of triumph. With her duplicitous husband tied helplessly in a chair, Paula lets out all her righteous anger. For the first time, she speaks her mind, boldly and clearly. For many, that is the sweetest wish-fulfillment ending of all.

The Piano
1993

With the grandeur of myth, the delicacy of fable, and the gravity of a morality play, *The Piano* is unique, dreamily strange, and often funny. It is a sensuous tale in which the object of erotic arousal is not a woman's body or fetishized body parts and clothes but her voice—her true inner voice. It is fitting that New Zealand director Jane Campion won an Oscar for her screenplay—her own inner voice.

Holly Hunter, who won an Oscar for her performance, plays a nineteenth-century Scottish mute named Ada. Even Ada does not know why she suddenly stopped speaking at an early age, although the movie implies that in a patriarchal society that doesn't let women speak for themselves and won't listen when they do, it's as if a woman simply doesn't have the means of speech at her disposal.

At first, we hear Ada's inner voice setting a few things out for us, and although we will not hear that voice again for a while, Ada has no problem communicating. She uses sign language with her ethereal daughter, Flora (Anna Paquin, who looked like a deer caught in headlights when her Oscar was announced). Flora interprets Ada—sometimes fancifully—to the outside world, making the daughter something of an extension of the mother. This symbiosis between mother and daughter is further heightened by their similar look; their faces are framed by a severe middle part in the hair and the hooded black bonnet of the day. Often the two bonnets bob and weave in synch.

When she must, Ada resorts to scribbling hasty, pointed messages on a pad hung around her neck. Otherwise, she uses body language and unusually expressive eyes; one sharp look is enough to discourage an advance or hush her daughter.

And then, of course, there is the piano, Ada's chief means of expression. She plays rapturously, and this is what initially seduces Baines

(Harvey Keitel), a white New Zealand settler who lives in harmony among the natives. Although Ada has been brought to the wilds in an arranged marriage with the hapless, unimaginative Stewart (Sam Neill), it is Baines who hears Ada's inner voice through the passion of her music.

Stewart has left the piano to rot on the beach, but Baines later has it hauled up the hill by the Maoris. Baines can neither read nor write, but he has the sensitivity to communicate with both the speechless Ada and the foreign-tongued locals.

In a Faustian bargain that ends up being exceptionally erotic, Baines lets Ada "buy back" her beloved instrument one black key at a time in return for "piano lessons." Baines doesn't really want to learn; he just wants to watch Ada play. It's a turn-on, but more than that, it's an emotional outlet for Baines. He takes further license with each lesson, at first merely looking up Ada's heavy skirts, then lying naked on his bed to watch.

To her husband Stewart, Ada is a cold "dwarf," but to Baines, she's the sensuous woman.

The piano lessons unleash Baines's own sensuality, to the point where he tenderly dusts the piano while in the nude, a scene as surprising for its full-frontal nudity of a known Hollywood star as for the honesty and sensitivity with which it handles the material. Audiences who find the scene erotic are not basing their reaction on the particulars of Keitel's middle-aged body but on how this pent-up, solitary character has been moved to such an emotionally naked, vulnerable place by a woman.

Similarly, when Ada sheds her clothes, we see a prim, stern, guarded character literally exposing herself for the first time, out from under massive and restrictive layers of clothing.

The final breakdown of civilization, at least in the eyes of Ada's husband, is when he observes his (bought and paid for) wife's infidelity with a man who not only lives among the natives but paints himself like one. Stewart cannot comprehend this betrayal of himself and his culture, even though he has failed to make any emotional connection with his wife. He wreaks revenge by chopping off one of Ada's fingers in what would be interpreted in a typical male director's movie as a gesture of emasculation. In the context of this film, however, it is really Ada's voice that he has gone after, since she has used those fingers to communicate her passion

Harvey Keitel is the only man who can hear Holly Hunter's inner voice and feel her passion in *The Piano*.

to Baines. In this movie, a woman's voice is far more powerful than a man's manhood, a subtext that perhaps unwittingly served to split the movie's supporters along gender lines. Stewart is not only jealous of the loss of his wife's sexual favors, he is far more furious that he has been so out of the loop that he cannot read a single signal from his wife.

Some viewers have wondered why Ada couldn't feel love for Stewart, who is not such a bad sort. The real reason, of course, is that he cannot "hear" her, but it's interesting how many viewers "forget" that Stewart twice attempts to rape his wife, once in the woods, where she clings horizontally to trees as he pulls at her legs, and once in her bed, while she is still unconscious after losing her finger. This second time, she opens her eyes just in time and flashes a distinct warning. Finally, Stewart hears her and heeds her and is so transported by hearing her inner voice that he finally sets her free.

By understanding his wife, Stewart finally gets what he wants — which, as it turns out, is not sex but an entrée into Ada's private world.

That Ada's mysterious lack of voice might be attributed to the smothering effects of the patriarchal society around her is given credence when she regains her voice through the agency of Baines. He is the first man in whom Ada finds a sympathetic ear, so to speak. Baines replaces her missing finger with a prosthesis, buys her a new piano, and restores her to a house not unlike the one we imagine she lived in with the father who sold her into marriage.

Once heard (and loved, respected, attended to, and with all the other accoutrements of being heard), Ada is free to speak again.

Someone to Watch Over Me
1987

Where is the shepherd for this lost lamb? Why, he may be sitting right outside your bedroom door, assigned to protect you.

As the title song and the opening panoramic view of a cold, sparkling Manhattan suggest, Mimi Rogers has everything money can buy except a strong man to watch over her and keep her safe. Luckily, new detective Tom Berenger has been assigned to do just that. What's better, he's taking the midnight shift, when a beautiful single woman can get lonely and scared.

Rogers plays impossibly wealthy socialite Claire Gregory in Ridley Scott's atmospheric thriller *Someone to Watch Over Me*. She moves and shakes in a high-end world of glamour, designer clothes, and meaningless cocktail chatter. Her wealthy boyfriend (John Rubenstein) uses his status to boss people around, since he has no intrinsic strength.

Claire is the only witness to a murder, and until she can testify against the nut job, she needs police protection around the clock. Enter Mike Keegan (Berenger), his first day on the job as a detective.

Mike is a reg'lar guy from blue-collar, working-class Queens. He has a wife (Lorraine Bracco) and kid and enjoys raucous beer parties with his cop pals. Director Scott sets up the worlds of his protagonists as if they were a universe apart, separated (not joined) by the Queensboro Bridge. On one end, a life of taste, breeding, elegance—plus a certain amount of phoniness. On the other, a life of money worries, tacky decor, braying accents—plus the invisible glue of family.

"If you're going to be my escort, you need a better tie," Claire tells Mike, making the limo stop at a fancy Fifth Avenue shop where she is known to everyone behind the counter by name.

The heady, expensive perfume of Claire's life addles Mike's brain. When he gets home, he views his surroundings with new eyes and sees the flaws. The movie is very much about class envy.

Socialite Mimi Rogers falls for attentive blue-collar hero Tom Berenger in *Someone to Watch Over Me;* **those all-nighters by her bedroom door are just too irresistible.**

Men may enjoy this movie because it shows a man's struggle between the humdrum routine of married life and the allure of penthouse sex. Women love it not only for its rescue fantasy but because it is the rare love triangle that lets them shift their alliances between the two women at will.

Though beautiful and tremulous, Claire is the less likable of the women. What does she do with her time in that endless Xanadu of a Fifth Avenue apartment? She has no visible means of support, never gets her hands dirty. She barely escapes the killer in her wobbly high heels and glitter stockings. But she has one thing every woman can relate to—a longing for someone to watch over her. Even the most self-sufficient women enjoy the white-knight fantasy of a strong, capable guy whose purpose in life is to guard and protect them. Nothing will ever happen to you on this man's watch.

Mike is a real man among the cocktail-party poseurs in Claire's life. He's socially awkward and not very educated. "These people are a bunch of screaming squirrels," he proclaims at a fancy soiree where he is picked over by the society ladies like a piece of choice meat. He mispronounces such words as "aperitif." But he's not afraid to come bursting into a public ladies' room to make sure Claire is unharmed. And the sight of Berenger's well-muscled arm lying protectively over Rogers's sleeping body, in her high-canopied bed, makes every female viewer feel as secure as if they had their own personal version of the Club.

Across the river and through the 'hoods is Ellie (Lorraine Bracco), hoisting groceries, washing windows, fixing carburetors, wearing sweatpants, and cursing like a sailor. You can't help liking Ellie; she calls it like she sees it. "Michael, my ass is falling," she complains, feeling the effects of age.

"I love that ass," he tells her. "Now get it into bed before it hits the ground."

She and Mike go to a restaurant that for their income bracket is very fancy. Ellie is thrilled. But Mike has already tasted better. Ellie sees that she cannot compete with the high-class goods and guesses that he's been unfaithful. "I want you to remember that I behaved like a lady, the kind of lady you apparently prefer," she screams at him in the parking lot before punching him in the mouth.

Someone to Watch Over Me came out the same year as *Fatal Attraction* and once again plays on society's fears of the sexually voracious single career woman. The movie ends with a piece of psychological viciousness, with Claire stumbling upon a family hugfest in which Mike, Ellie, and their son are clinging to each other so tightly you'd think the nuclear family were under nuclear attack. There is no place for Claire here, in Queens, where real people live.

We last see Claire wearing some other cop's jacket for warmth, no doubt continuing her endless search for someone to watch over her. One of the reasons the wife is triumphant, after all, is that she proclaims, "I can take care of myself!" And she proves it by shooting the perp to death right there in her kitchen, in defense of home and hearth.

Apparently, having someone to watch over you is not just a fantasy for females.

Summertime

1955

It's never too late for love.

"No one's older than me," complains old maid Jane Hudson (Katharine Hepburn). Her Venetian landlady insists that age is an asset in Italy, where Jane has come for a once-in-a-lifetime vacation. "Then I'm loaded," she concludes bitterly.

Jane is middle-aged and a virgin. When she returns to her hotel late and finds people worried about her, she reassures them: "No, nothing happened to me. That's my history."

Venice, as gloriously filmed by director David Lean, is filled with mystery, promise, and lovers. Everywhere Jane goes, there are couples snuggling. She films everything with her camera, always recording but never living. She tells her landlady about a "girl" she met on the way over, "a girl wanting to come to Europe to find something," she says, fooling no one. "Way back in the back of her mind was something she was looking for, a wonderful, mystical, magical miracle. . . . I guess to find what she's been missing all her life."

If what she's been missing is sex, she has come to the right place. "Those miracles, they can happen sometimes," promises the landlady.

Within a few minutes on the Piazza San Marco, dapper shopkeeper Renato Di Rossi (Rossano Brazzi) has noticed Jane's nicely turned ankle. A quickie romance ensues, hampered by Jane's fear and inexperience, not to mention cultural differences. "The most beautiful things in life are things we do not understand," says Renato in his aggressive wooing of Jane. "We saw each other, we liked each other. . . . This is so nice, how can it be wrong?"

It can easily be wrong. Renato has neglected to tell Jane that he is married with children; oops! Jane is *shocked* to learn this. She also senses that it may be her last chance to "find what she's been missing all her life,"

Married Italian shopkeeper Rossano Brazzi is Katharine Hepburn's one last chance to lose her virginity in *Summertime*.

and that's too precious to throw away. When the gardenia Renato has given her drifts away on the water, we know virginity is soon to follow.

Love and its earthly delights turns Jane into a Cinderella in ball-gown finery and red high heels. She and her lover embrace on a balcony as fireworks explode overhead, and one red shoe is left behind. Jane is going to get her prince before she's turned back into a pumpkin.

The appeal of *Summertime* is easy to understand. Middle-aged women rarely get a chance at love in the movies. If not for the exotic locale, these two could be any working-class couple, the secretary and the shopkeeper, enjoying thrills that are usually the preserve of the young and wealthy.

David Lean made *Summertime* ten years after *Brief Encounter*, another movie about a last chance for middle-aged, middle-class love. Both movies end with trains taking one of the partners away, for love like this is meant to be a midlife injection of vitamin B_{12} and not much more.

"You and I would end in nothing," says Jane. "All my life I've stayed at parties too long because I didn't know when to go. Now, with you, I've grown up. I think I do know when to go."

Jane gracefully withdraws from her passion before it is revealed to be not the antique red vase she thought it was but just another tourist item with a markup. She waves to Renato as her train pulls away, waves and waves like a bird taking off.

BAD GIRLS

Just as villains are intrinsically more interesting than heroes, bad girls are more fun than good girls. They do things with impunity most women can only daydream about, and they act of their own volition instead of following society's rigid rules concerning female deportment. But in what ways are movie vixens really so bad? Anne Parillaud in *La Femme Nikita* is less threatening to society once she learns to use makeup and smile through her anger. Lana Turner and, in the remake, Jessica Lange are frustrated wives who kill only after feeling suffocated in *The Postman Always Rings Twice*. Jessica Lange is punished in *Frances* for the sin of doing and saying as she pleases. And Rita Hayworth in *Gilda* makes no apologies for the good times she's had or the company she's kept. The only truly rotten of these bad girls is Linda Fiorentino in *The Last Seduction*, and she's so rotten she's adorable.

Anne Parillaud is a dangerous weapon for the French government in *La Femme Nikita* once she's learned the art of being totally feminine. Oh, yes, and how to shoot a gun.

La Femme Nikita
1991

At the height of the killer-babe movement in movies, along came *La Femme Nikita*, in which an unregenerate nineteen-year-old junkie is turned into a government assassin in black mini and stiletto heels. Women love it.

We don't love it for the same reasons as men, even though it is a kick to see a teenager so tough and anarchic that she can calmly shoot a police officer in the face. Women are brought up to be so careful of others that they often apologize when someone else bumps into them; it's liberating to watch a female character blithely stab a cop through the hand with a pencil.

The incorrigible Nikita (Anne Parillaud) is arrested, tried, and sentenced to death. She is given a presumably lethal injection. Then she wakes up in a bright, subterranean cell, having been shanghaied into a secret program that gives the most hardened death-row inmates one last chance—as a hired gun for the French government.

The girl is subjected to a strenuous makeover on all fronts: She must learn computers, self-defense, firearms, and also makeup and deportment. It's a finishing school for killers.

But Nikita does not go gently into that good afterlife. She kicks, screams, and bites. Even the estimable Jeanne Moreau, playing Nikita's grande-dame instructor in feminine charms, cannot get the child to use the right fork or to smile winsomely.

Nikita passes her final exam when she is taken to a ritzy restaurant for her twenty-third birthday; it's her first time in the real world since her incarceration. She is dressed to the nines, which means more thigh than skirt. Her birthday present, unwrapped during a champagne toast, is an automatic weapon that comes with instructions to kill a man seated at a nearby table. If she can kill him and get out of the restaurant alive, she graduates.

Thereafter, Nikita makes a kind of double life for herself, enjoying domestic bliss with her blissfully unaware boyfriend (Jean-Hugues Anglade) while occasionally going out on a government job. As it is for any working woman, it's not easy to balance love and career. Even a romantic vacation in Venice is compromised; while the boyfriend is pledging his troth in the hotel room, Nikita has holed up in the bathroom by the window with a high-powered rifle, waiting for her mark.

The movie, directed by Luc Besson, did unusually big business in the United States and was remade in Hollywood in 1993 with Bridget Fonda as *Point of No Return.* The remake, though inferior in other ways, does manage to underscore that which is of most interest to the female audience—how girls get dragged into womanhood kicking and screaming.

Anne Parillaud played Nikita as a feral social reject whose carnality and femininity can, with practice, be harnessed. Bridget Fonda's "Maggie" is a different kind of menace to society—the kind of woman who is threatening because she doesn't wear makeup or shave under her arms. Both ladies are of use to their governments (and to society in general) only when they can be as quick with a lipstick as with a loaded gun.

In the remake, Maggie is more clearly defined as a tomboy who, in order to learn about love, must give up her fusion with mother (Maggie won't even discuss her mother, although she plainly longs for her) and transfer her attachment to father. The father figure is her instructor, Bob (Gabriel Byrne), who teaches Maggie everything she needs to know and serves as her first love object. The next step to womanhood is to leave him ("That's the last time I'll ever kiss you," she tells Bob) in order to form a healthier attachment to a real boyfriend (gentle, befuddled Dermot Mulroney).

The free-spirited wild child is easily able to master the fundamentals of karate and computers. Ladylike behavior, on the other hand, must be force-fed. The Jeanne Moreau character is played in the remake by Anne Bancroft, who delivers a series of grueling deportment lessons. Bancroft is the putative "mother" who turns wistful when seeing her fully transformed "daughter" leave home on her first date. She ruefully completes Maggie's indoctrination by teaching her those bizarre "essentials" that society prizes: the woman who can contain her anger by smiling when she'd rather hit.

The "intuitive" behavior of femininity is lampooned throughout the remake. In the kitchen, where Maggie is particularly inept, she wields a huge cleaver; in fact, she escapes a restaurant kitchen in a hail of bullets — it's dangerous to renounce womanhood. When set loose in a supermarket, she has no idea how to shop. Even flirting is a learned skill.

Maggie learns easily, but she cannot quite become what the men want her to be; hence, her conflict. She won't be turned into a Stepford wife, even though the rewards for prettiness and good behavior are plentiful.

Bob's superior officer is the only one to realize that Maggie is resistant to brainwashing. He tells a sexist joke, and when Maggie refuses to laugh, he turns on her: "I think you're dangerous."

At the end of the movie, when Bob fudges a report to his boss — "The girl's dead," he says, letting her get away — he is partly correct in the sense that the girl is dead. Long live the woman.

Frances

1982

Frances Farmer was a headstrong, left-leaning young actress with a promising future in the 1930s. She landed a few minor roles, including one opposite Bing Crosby in *Come and Get It*. Emotional instability did her in, and after numerous bouts with the nuthouse and finally a lobotomy, Frances was finally brought under control, her career kaput.

Her story is dramatically and rather depressingly chronicled in *Frances*, one of Jessica Lange's two movies in 1982. As the hot new thing, Lange was nominated for both movies, winning a supporting Oscar for *Tootsie*, although it was her lead in *Frances* that she cared for more passionately. Making the movie was a labor of love, with her real-life boyfriend Sam Shepard playing the one man who perhaps could have saved Frances from herself. As it was, this serious prestige movie all but cried out for the box office to hang a Gone Fishin' sign.

Yet women love this movie with a soap-opera zeal. Thanks to Lange's interpretation, *Frances* became the story of a daughter who failed to make the most crucial break of a girl's life—separating from her mother. And is she ever punished for it.

Frances's mom (Kim Stanley) is a self-deluded, bitter woman who, having failed to be a somebody in her own life, piggybacks all her frustrated ambitions onto the success of her daring but emotionally fragile daughter.

Frances is a free spirit who speaks her mind from a young age. In high school, she wins an essay contest with a paean to atheism that scandalizes the neighbors. Torn between her overweening mother and her weak-willed dad, Frances grows up rebellious but always in thrall to Mom. She has no social skills (or refuses to employ them) to mitigate the force of her words in a conservative society. Whether telling a cop to

Jessica Lange is led away to the nuthouse as punishment for having a mind of her own and speaking it in *Frances*.

fuck himself or defying accepted rules of conduct for ladies, Frances alienates male society at every turn.

"You give 'em what they want, you can have anything," her occasional lover (Shepard) tells her.

"I don't have what they want," she replies.

Therein lies one of Frances's problems: There's nothing wrong with her that changing the expectations of others can't solve. The studio boss wants her to be prompt and docile. Her coworkers want her to leave their hypocrisy unexamined. Her short-lived marriage to an actor (in real life, Leif Erickson) would have worked if only she'd been the sort of woman who would not leave her weaker husband behind professionally. Frances was many things, but not the answer to the prayers of 1930s men.

Frances can be seen as a movie about how the Hollywood system of yore could chew 'em up and spit 'em out. But its resonance for ordinary women is the eternal mother-daughter power struggle. In return for defying her mother, Frances is locked up in an insane asylum, where she is drugged, tied to a bed, and gang-raped by servicemen who bribe the night watchman. Anything Frances says on her own behalf is suspect. Her already high strung nature frays from a barrage of deceit and betrayal. The movie presents an exceptional, spirited young woman who is punished for having a will of her own.

Not since Joe Kennedy's daughter had a lobotomy has that operation seemed so ill advised. As a surgeon smugly puts it, a lobotomy results in "emotional flattening, with diminished creativity and imagination." Naturally, Frances is not consulted beforehand.

After the operation, Frances is a docile, boring creature. The way she spouts platitudes sounds much like the traditional feminine ideal, as if the lobotomy accomplished a kind of forced cultural mainstreaming. Frances is now manageable and therefore a success in the eyes of Mom and society at large. But she has lost all that made her special. Only when she was a bad girl was she a real person.

Early in her career, Frances sneaks away from a stifling movie premiere to breathe the night air with Shepard, the only honest person in her life. He never bullshits her. After the lobotomy, she asks him how she looks, and although he is just as horrified by her transformation as the audience, he lies to her for the first time. "You always look like a million bucks," he says. That is the moment when Frances realizes she has lost everything of value.

When her sarcasm is lost on an asylum shrink, the camera does a close-up of the man shaving his pencil to a point. It's not as if Frances is oblivious of the way society is whittling her down; she just doesn't have the strength or means to withstand it. "You're trying to break my spirit," she yells at her mother. "You're trying to turn me into you!"

That sound is the rustle of the attentive female audience, nodding to themselves, nervously checking their own pulses. To be a bad girl may be the only way to stay alive.

Gilda

1946

"Are you decent?" asks Gilda's new husband, Ballin Mundson, as he enters her bedroom with Johnny Farrell, his trusted assistant.

"Me?" she asks, flinging her flaming hair back over her shoulders, face aglow. It's one of the red-hot double entendres that keeps *Gilda* percolating.

This is the movie that made Rita Hayworth a star. She plays a girl so bad that an awkward ending was tacked on to appease the censors and provide a kind of disclaimer. She did none of those things you think she did, Johnny Farrell is told. But he is told this in such a hurried whisper that we can disregard it the way we would twin beds in a love nest. Gilda is a slut! The girl can't help it!

Anyway, it's not because she's bought and paid for that Gilda is the odd man out in *Gilda*. The homosexual subtext between casino owner Ballin (George Macready) and Johnny (Glenn Ford) is so thick that you could run it through with a sword hidden in a cane—the same phallic sword that Ballin shows Johnny when they meet one night on the Buenos Aires wharf and which they later toast as their "friend." They promise each other there will be no women to disrupt their union, and Johnny rises in the ranks at the casino to become the manager.

When Ballin returns from a mysterious trip with a wife in tow, Johnny acts like a scorned lover; in fact, it's clear he once knew Gilda quite well himself.

Hate is such an exciting emotion, as Ballin points out, and thereafter in this movie the words "hate" and "love" are interchangeable. Despite the homosexual subtext, women can read the movie the traditional way, with Johnny torn between loyalty to his employer and his reawakened passion. Gilda offers a toast to the woman who brought him to this impasse. "Let's hate her!" she proposes.

Don't put the blame on Mame, boys. Who is Rita Hayworth to fill her dance card with in *Gilda* if her hubby is more interested in spending quality time with her ex?

Female audiences forcibly stick to an interpretation of the movie that keeps Gilda front and center. But it's hard to ignore a subtext that screams for recognition. Johnny really does hate Gilda, because she has come between him and his real love, which is the boss man and his, uh, sword. When faced with whether to bail out Gilda at the bar or attend to Ballin in the office, Johnny hesitates, then runs upstairs to the office. "Now we know," says the omniscient washroom attendant.

There is another possibility for interpretation that allows the discriminating female viewer to eat her cake and have it, too. Just as Ballin can be considered a closet homosexual who makes nighttime visits to the waterfront, Johnny can be viewed as a closet heterosexual who is frustrated because Gilda has an uncanny ability to arouse him. She looks down at his pants and notes this meaningfully as they share a dance. Her flirtations with Johnny can be seen as taunting him about his masculinity; hence, the slap he gives her after her aborted public striptease to "Put the Blame on Mame."

Whichever direction the love triangle takes, *Gilda* is a provocatively sadistic movie. Gilda flaunts her sexuality and walks off with just about any guy who'll buy her a drink. (Of course, being the boss's wife, her drinks are free.) Johnny dutifully chauffeurs her to these hotel assignations because he treats her like "the laundry." (Like Ballin's personal laundry, that is. And Johnny, of all people, should be familiar with Ballin's personal laundry.)

"Did you teach her to swim?" Ballin asks suspiciously when Johnny brings Gilda home after hours with the lame excuse that they went swimming.

"I taught her everything she knows," he snaps, back in double entendreville. Even so, it's more likely that Gilda taught Johnny everything *he* knows, which would explain why he can't get over her dumping him.

Story line and hidden intrigue aside, Hayworth is so sexy and dazzling that what woman would not like to be her, tramp or no? She unabashedly cheats on both husband and ex-lover. When she sees that Johnny is watching her jealously, she pulls closer the dance partner she just got through chiding for feeling her up. "Where most dancers move from the hips down, Hayworth moves from the knees up, her shoulders drawn back, projecting her breast cage forward in the most enticing manner, only acceptable in the young and very beautiful," said choreographer Jack Cole, as reported in Otto Friedrich's book *City of Nets*.

Women idolize Gilda for the apparent ease with which she uses her body both for her own pleasure and to entice men. The idea of two men fighting over her provides that all-important ego rush.

Johnny treats Gilda horrifically, refusing to sleep with her when they are later married and keeping her under lock and key. Yet his sadism can be viewed through the rose-colored sunglasses of the battered-wife syndrome: He must really love her an awful lot to be so cruel.

Everything we see as romantic about *Gilda* is in fact a bit perverted, even from behind the scenes. Hayworth was shy little Margarita Carmen Dolores Cansino from Jackson Heights, Queens. Her remarkable ability to dance and seem sexually knowledgeable brought her a lifetime of older men who turned her into the fiction of Rita Hayworth. They changed her name, dyed her hair, even forced her to undergo two years of electrolysis to raise her feral hairline. Columbia studio boss Harry Cohn was obsessed with her and hid microphones in her dressing room to monitor her conversations with Glenn Ford, an actor who was brought into the picture after filming had already begun. Later, of course, Orson Welles married and then divorced her, but not before he punitively hacked off her beautiful locks for *The Lady From Shanghai*.

"Every man I've known has fallen in love with Gilda," Hayworth complained years later, "and wakened with me." Bad girls do pay a price.

The Last Seduction

1994

The old days of film noir featured sirens on whose rocky shoals the heroes crashed. Linda Fiorentino goes those sirens one decibel better in *The Last Seduction*, playing an *Über*-bitch who must have been born without an amygdala, the portion of the brain that governs emotion.

She plays Bridget Gregory in director John Dahl's neonoir. Bridget is so bad, she stubs out her cigarette in the apple pie grandma baked. And she's so good, men will do anything to please her—even commit murder.

Bridget is a woman of unbridled chutzpah who has never met a man she couldn't grind beneath her four-inch heel. She steals her husband's drug-deal money ("You shouldn't have slapped me!" she rationalizes) and then goes on the lam, trying to blend in with the rubes of a small town in upstate New York.

The minute she strides into a crowded bar, local hayseed Mike (Peter Berg) is smitten. "I'm hung like a horse," he boasts, trying to match her air of authority. "Let's see, Mr. Ed," she retorts coolly, putting her hand in his pants.

Mike makes the cut. After sex, he gets all soft and cuddly toward her, the stereotype of how women warm to their men after orgasm. In this cartoon of gender role reversal, Bridget is barely even amused by Mike's emotional vulnerability. No sooner have her toes uncurled than she is already on to the next item on her agenda. She hardly remembers that there's someone still warming the bed.

Mike does have his uses. He comes in handy as a front for Bridget while she's avoiding that angry husband. And he's so malleable that he barely protests when Bridget pulls the old Barbara Stanwyck routine on him.

"I won't commit murder!" he says weakly.

"You would if you loved me," says Bridget, pouting.

Bridget toys with a deadly entrepreneurial idea involving telephone

Linda Fiorentino may not have a heartbeat, but she knows how to play men's heartstrings like a pro in *The Last Seduction*.

solicitation. She cold-calls women to tell them their husbands are cheating on them, then plants the idea that they could collect big insurance bucks should something unfortunate happen to the cad. To be fair, the movie tips its cloche to *Double Indemnity*, the first movie to prove that insurance agents aren't all so predictable. There's a reference to the name Neff—as in Walter Neff, the sappy insurance salesman who was undone by Stanwyck's ankle strap.

Fiorentino's bitch-vixen is so cartoonishly over the top that men and women can laugh along. Meanwhile, the women feel a secret glee over Bridget's intelligence and power. We even enjoy her lack of emotion. What a relief it would be (in the abstract, that is) to have a moment's peace from all that emotional baggage!

Bridget cunningly wears Mike's shirt, knowing he is looking for clues of her love. "Where does this leave me?" he whimpers. "You're my designated fuck," she whips back, part of Steve Barancik's razor-sharp and decadently funny script.

Bill Pullman plays the equally untrustworthy husband whose thumbs Bridget leaves to the loan sharks after she steals the money he was going to use to pay them off. ("Anyone checked you for a heartbeat lately?" asks J. T. Walsh, her amused lawyer.)

Although the action takes place in the town Bridget derides as "Mayberry," New York is a player, or at least a specter. It is Bridget's big-city nerves of steel that attract Mike. Bridget uses small-town psychology to manipulate the locals—she plays on Mike's fears of being a hayseed—while the New Yorker in her finds it hard to say "please" and "thank you."

The big-city professional woman may be seen as threatening, but Bridget's pride in her own power over men is nearly as intoxicating to the audience as having such power firsthand.

The Postman Always Rings Twice
1946, 1981

The sign outside the roadside diner says Man Wanted, and once you see glamorous Lana Turner idling her time away as chief short-order cook and bottle washer, you can guess who posted it. In the original 1946 version of *The Postman Always Rings Twice*, drifter John Garfield is the man she wants.

This steamy movie of illicit passion and bungled murder was based on the James M. Cain potboiler and features elements also found in Cain's *Double Indemnity*—a suspicious insurance policy, a love triangle, and a loser brought low by his lust for a bad woman.

Like most bad women, Cora Smith (Turner) isn't *totally* bad. She's just bored. As the wife of Greek diner owner Nick Smith (Cecil Kellaway), Cora wears virginal white and even has a change of heart near the end of the movie. Viewers can more or less forgive her for wanting her silly, drunken husband out of the way, especially once they see the chemistry between Turner and Garfield.

"Do you love me, Cora?" asks the hard-bitten Garfield once he is under her spell. "Yes, you do," he answers for her in a telling bit of circular logic. "You couldn't get me to agree to a thing like this if you didn't."

Just as in *Double Indemnity*, we first meet the lady of the house from her ankles up. In this case, the camera catches Turner's lipstick first as it rolls on the floor. Then the camera travels up her legs in a kind of "pantyhose cam." Cora is always dolled up, her lipstick and platinum hair just so, a glamour queen who wants the opportunity to make more of herself than her marriage of convenience has offered her.

It's the sexual chemistry that made *Postman* such a hit, earning a respectable $4 million during its initial release. Narrated by the Garfield character in flashback, the movie presents his side of the story. But female viewers have no trouble identifying with the stifled housewife who can

Lana Turner knows what she wants, and John
Garfield will go to any lengths to get it for her in the
1946 version of *The Postman Always Rings Twice*.

find no outlet other than infidelity. When the husband announces his uni-
lateral decision to sell the diner and move to northern Canada, where
Cora will be expected to spend her vibrant years ministering to an invalid
sister-in-law, the audience is horrified. Men may see *Postman* as a morality tale about being brought low by a bad girl, but women see it as about
someone who is unjustly penalized for having, and acting on, desires of
her own. To Cora, marriage is a prison with no parole.

Tough-guy actor Garfield gives a typically physical performance. But
the actor, who died six years later of a heart attack after being black-
listed, had just been dismissed from military service for "a bum ticker,"

Postman came out two years after *Double Indemnity*—also based on a James M. Cain novel and sharing many similarities—with married Barbara Stanwyck luring Fred MacMurray to his doom.

according to the *Motion Picture Guide*. Director Tay Garnett had to chase after him all the time to keep Garfield from playing handball during his breaks. "Don't get me wrong," Garnett is said to have told him. "I don't want to louse up your fun, but I've got to finish this picture."

The 1946 version proved steamy enough, but the Production Code made sure everything was left to the imagination. Bob Rafelson's 1981 remake took the sex more literally, turning *Postman* into a feeding frenzy of lust between drifter Jack Nicholson and a deglamorized Jessica Lange. In this version, the subtext of a woman's freedom from a stifling marriage is no longer the drawing card for female audiences. Now it's about sexual satisfaction.

The set piece of the remake comes early on when Frank Chambers nearly rapes Cora the first time he's alone with her. "Wait!" she cries from the kitchen table, where he has thrown her. Covered in flour, she shoves a newly baked bread and a carving knife off the table, and the two go at it most graphically. There are close-ups of Nicholson's hand and mouth on Lange's pubis. When they bash each other about in order to give themselves alibis for the husband's car going off a cliff, they are so turned on by the fisticuffs that they pause for an implausible quickie in the bushes.

Frank has an affair in the remake with a traveling circus performer, played by Nicholson's offscreen lover at the time, Anjelica Huston. The "exotic" nature of the interlude is a good example of what plays only to a male audience—sex in a van with a lion tamer and her cats. What's more interesting (and poignant) to women is when Cora, having just decided to trust again, realizes she's been betrayed.

Both movies are about how love can only survive when there's trust. "There's always a way, Cora, if you stick together," chides Frank early on. Every time the lovers doubt each other, they wander further off the path, until they are so riven with doubt that a happy ending is impossible. The moral is that murdering your husband is neither here nor there but not trusting your lover is a sin.

HUNKS

Most movies contain visual aids for male viewers—scenes improbably set in strip clubs, with scantily clad bimbos cast as extras or girlfriends. Women are visual creatures, too, and they've proven it by supporting movies with cute guys in the lead. It helps if they're sweetly insecure, like Patrick Swayze in *Dirty Dancing* or William Holden in *Picnic*; if they're emotionally torn, like Harrison Ford in *Witness*; if they're studly and proud of it, like Paul Newman in *Hud*; or if there's a chance to reform them, like Richard Gere in *American Gigolo*. If they take off their clothes and stretch, that can only be a plus.

As Julian the *American Gigolo*, Richard Gere makes older women happy and Giorgio Armani a household name. His appeal is that maybe the right woman can change him.

American Gigolo

1980

When he gets up naked from the bed and strolls to the window to pronounce his philosophy of life—that is, the pleasuring of older women—it is Richard Gere's finest hour.

Not as an actor, perhaps, since his performance in *American Gigolo* is rather cold. But as a sex symbol, what a lovely vision. The first American star to do casual full-frontal nudity in a Hollywood movie, Gere exhibits a three-quarter profile while pontificating on how it took him three hours to get one older woman to climax. "Who else would have taken the time?" he asks, as if he were Hamlet pondering action. "Who else would do it right?"

John Travolta had been offered *American Gigolo*, but his price was too high. He and Gere had started out together on Broadway in *Grease*, and although Gere had the better role, Travolta won out for the movie version, thereby eclipsing Gere professionally for the next few years.

American Gigolo is all style over substance. Clothing makes the man—as do music, lighting, and mood—in writer-director Paul Schrader's drama about a classy male prostitute who is framed for murder.

The murder is the maguffin. This movie is all about Richard Gere's body, and it deliberately plays to women. Not to the lonely, wealthy matrons Schrader imagines as the potential clients for such a man but to younger women who can fantasize warming that cold heart and leading him away from a life of passionless sex.

We never actually see what it is that makes Julian such a great hustler. He doesn't do gay sex or "kink"; he has scruples about handcuffs and sex toys. But hey, we believe him when he sizes up one woman in bed and tells her with utmost authority: "I know you're going to like me."

Aside from Gere's gorgeous face and body, the appeal of Julian's character is twofold. The important thing about his sexual prowess isn't that he's so good at it, as he continually boasts, but that he takes responsibility. "Leave everything to me; I know what you need," he says. Even sexually aggressive women find this reassuring; there's no turn-off like a sexually insecure man.

The second factor is that Julian, the most unattainable man in town because he is so readily available to anyone who pays, has an Achilles heel that makes him winnable, after all. Lauren Hutton finds that Achilles heel and kicks it hard. "You could have forgotten me!" Julian says from behind glass in the jail where Hutton has come to shore up his alibi, at the expense of her marriage and reputation. "I'd rather die," she tells him.

And then the immortal words: "Oh, my God, Michelle," says Julian. "It's taken me so long to come to you!"

Of course, it's not very believable under the circumstances. He's only known her a few weeks, so it hasn't taken him *that* long to come to her. And the more skeptical will wonder why a hustler says that immediately after the woman offers him an alibi that will save his skin.

Even if these qualities didn't make Julian a dreamboat—the perfect lover who is ready to renounce infidelity—think of it this way. It's hard to find a man who cares that much about his wardrobe.

Armani, by the way.

Dirty Dancing
1987

Many a bored daughter has spent her vacation wondering how to get away from her parents and shuffleboard and win the heart of the one stud on the premises. *Dirty Dancing* works that fantasy, baby.

The stud teaching cha-cha at Kellerman's Catskills resort is Patrick Swayze, and is he a sight! Among all the nerdy Ivy League–bound boys who wait tables for the summer and boast of their credentials, Swayze is a hunk of genuine raw meat. He has the physical self-assurance that makes crowds part for him — which is handy, because he dances with such explosive sexual energy that he often needs just such a runway.

Playing Johnny Castle, misunderstood mambo man, was Swayze's big career break. All his movies since then have been built on the same promise — that underneath that exciting athlete's body with the trained dancer's grace lies a man that even a wallflower can conquer.

Jennifer Grey plays the wallflower, a skinny, awkward, unprepossessing Jewish teenager everyone still refers to as "Baby."

It's the summer of 1963, the summer before great social upheaval on the landscape and a time when Baby "never thought I'd find a guy as great as Daddy." From the first moment she sees Johnny on the dance floor, Daddy is history.

Baby acts around Johnny the way any smitten teen would. When he meets her eyes, she gulps air. When she speaks to him, she says something incredibly stupid. And when he takes her cardboard-stiff body in his arms to show her how to do the "dirty dancing" that rules in the staff quarters after-hours, she mistakes it for a personal interest in her. It's an understandable mistake, but let's face it. Johnny is paid to show the female customers a good time, either with a dance card or his room key. Tips are welcome.

The dancing in *Dirty Dancing* is a clear metaphor for sex, made all the more transparent by Kenny Ortega's joyfully body conscious choreography. When Baby peeks in at the staff quarters, which are off-limits to guests, she sees the equivalent of a basement make-out session. The boys and girls are all swooning in each other's arms with sexual abandon, humping each other's legs and pelvises, grinding away. Baby knows she has seen something secret and special. It's not the staff that's off-limits, really; it's their secret knowledge of each other's bodies.

The story has two big problems to work out as far as an anxious female audience is concerned. First, how could a plain, inexperienced girl like Baby interest the Big Man on Campus? And second, even if Baby could bed him (or dance with him) once, how could she keep his interest when he has better, prettier, or richer partners to choose from? What would set her apart from the bored fiftysomethings who pay him for private, horizontal mambo lessons whenever hubby is out of town?

Well, Baby has something a lesser person doesn't—great determination. To help out Johnny's chief (and conveniently platonic) dancing partner, Penny (Cynthia Rhodes), Baby learns the steps to a big mambo routine coming up. At first, she learns by rote. But the steps aren't enough, she's told; you've gotta *feel* the music. Baby's virginal body doesn't know how to respond to these sexual cues.

There is a point later in the movie in which she goes to bed with Johnny, but in the movie's subtext, Baby loses her virginity during the famous "bridge" montage, which shows her practicing, practicing, practicing, gradually getting looser and sexier. She changes to a midriff blouse. Her cutoff shorts get shorter. After a threesome, in which Johnny guides her from the front and Penny from behind (thus tacitly giving Baby permission to take Penny's man), Baby is next seen on that bridge taking a languorous breather and applying lipstick. *Now* she gets it, thank you very much. *Now* she feels that heartbeat Johnny is always trying to pound into her.

This takes care of getting the wallflower into position as someone a Johnny Castle could possibly take to bed.

But for Johnny to love her, to come back to her even after being fired from the resort, to have the motivation and gall to reintroduce Baby to her own father by her given name of Frances—for this, the screenwriter had to devalue the man behind the image. There was no other way to make it work.

It turns out that Johnny is insecure. *Terribly insecure*. He's afraid that women are using him for his body. (Well, they are.) He's lower class, uneducated, misunderstood—and oh, how he suffers over this. Only Baby, with her unique powers of compassion and insight, can understand him.

"Most of all I'm scared of walking out of this door and never feeling my whole life the way I feel with you," admits Baby in her big moment of emotional truth, a scene that would send a man with less insecurity scurrying out the door. Then she asks him to dance with her, and she couldn't be more explicit if she used the "f" word.

Even after learning to dance, Baby still has a problem with lifts, which in context we can read as orgasm. By the end of the movie, she can jump into Johnny's arms and be held aloft, thus achieving the final glory of the dirty dance.

Now, *that's* the summer vacation of which young girls dream.

Patrick Swayze teaches Jennifer Grey how to do the horizontal mambo and other fancy steps in *Dirty Dancing*.

Hud

1963

Hud's a bad guy—or as his daddy's housekeeper tells him, "You're an unprincipled man, Hud." And we love him for it.

Paul Newman, at the height of his attractiveness, manages to play the unprincipled louse Hud Bannon like a guy any woman would want to take home and tame. Partly it's the way Newman plays him, like a man hurting inside who needs to mask the pain with sex and booze and self-destructive behavior. And partly it's the way Newman fills out those tank-top under-shirts when he's working the ranch or winning a pig-wrestling contest.

What kind of name is Hud, anyway? Its internal rhyme suggests "hunk" or "stud," and he is just that. He's Melvyn Douglas's one surviv-ing son, the one no one can control. When there's a sick animal on the ranch, Hud's nephew (Brandon de Wilde) is dispatched to find which married woman's house Hud might be in. "You got no check on your appetites at all," his daddy tells Hud with disdain, although female audi-ences eat that up with a spoon. No check on his appetites, huh? Who wouldn't like the challenge of feeding him till he was sated?

With the cattle all quarantined because of possible hoof-and-mouth disease—in which case they will all be shot—Hud sees his chances for inheritance slipping away. He hates his father because he thinks his dad blames him for the death of his brother. This notion is not far wrong. Yet instead of siding with the father and his righteous pain, we feel for Hud. The poor guy, suffering all that guilt! "My mama loved me, but she died," Hud says bluntly.

Patricia Neal plays the older woman in Hud's life, the no-nonsense housekeeper Alma Brown. She is the only female Hud has not been able to seduce.

Alma once had a bad marriage before coming to live at the Bannon household. "Don't go shooting all the dogs just because one of them's got fleas," says Hud, flirting with her on her bed.

"I was married to Ed for six years. Only thing he was ever good for was scratching my back where I couldn't reach it."

"Ya still got that itch?" asks Hud, glancing pointedly at her crotch.

"Off and on."

"Well, lemme know when it gets ta botherin' ya."

The audience wants Hud to be tamed and hopes it will be by Alma, who, as an older and far from glamorous woman, offers no threat to the audience. Instead, Hud gets drunk and frustrated and tries to rape Alma when he could have had her with a little patience and a change in attitude.

In the end, Hud is left all alone. He pulls a window shade halfway down, and the pull string swings like a mininoose, the one he has metaphorically hung around his own neck.

Paul Newman is trouble in *Hud*, but who can resist? Not a lady in town except for housekeeper Patricia O'Neal, the only woman who could have saved him.

The character of Hud—whose mama loved him but died—arouses both the maternal, nurturing instincts of the audience and also a primal sexual desire. "The only question I ever ask is What time is your husband coming home," Hud boasts.

No wonder in such a small town there is no dearth of married women who would risk their necks for a one-night stand with Hud, the flea-bitten dog that every woman wants to groom.

Picnic
1955

"He clomped through the place like it was still outdoors" is how one elderly neighbor thinks back on William Holden's twenty-four-hour visit to the small Kansas town. "There was a *man* in the house, and it seemed good."

Every female within miles is swooning with lust over Holden, who plays handsome drifter Hal Carter in *Picnic*. There is some reason in nearly every scene for him to take his shirt off, "naked as an Indian," as "old-maid-schoolteacher" Rosalind Russell refers to him.

Hal hops a train into town in search of a wealthy college buddy (Cliff Robertson). First he stops to do some yard work in return for a meal and a wash, and that's where he spies the sisters Owens, lovely Madge (Kim Novak) and brainy Millie (Susan Strasberg). He bounces a basketball off the head of a geeky teenager who is trying to pick up Madge. "Who are you?" demands the local boy. "What's *that* matter? I'm bigger'n you," says Hal, reeking of testosterone.

Beauty is the hot topic in the all-female Owens house. Madge is tired of being prized only for her looks. Younger sister Millie is tired of never being prized for hers. Their frustrated mother (Betty Field), having missed her own opportunities, keeps egging Madge on to use her looks to marry well. And the schoolmarm boarder is desperately afraid of aging.

Hal's arrival on Labor Day—the last official day of summer and the last chance for most of the characters—shakes things up.

Everyone goes off to the annual picnic in high spirits. Hal's college buddy turns out to be Madge's boyfriend, who promises Hal a lowly job at his dad's grain factory. Hal borrows his friend's jacket but has to take it off. "I'm kinda beefy through the shoulders."

This beefiness through the shoulders does not go unnoticed. "He carries that old washtub as if it were so much tissue paper," marvels the old

Willam Holden's bare chest makes Labor Day sizzle in a small Kansas town in *Picnic*. **It's enough to cause a healthy rift between Kim Novak and her mother.**

lady from next door. The women panic whenever Hal stands too close to them. You can practically feel their skin tingle.

Madge feels an immediate attraction. Her mother melts when Hal gives her the eye and makes her feel young again. The "old-maid school-teacher" gets drunk at the picnic and, feeling the weight of her spinster-hood, practically claws Hal's shirt off. He reminds her, she says, of "one of those old statues, a Roman gladiator," wearing only a shield. When he rejects her, she turns on him, accusing him of "strutting around like some crummy Apollo!"

Everyone sees right through Hal—he is uncouth, boastful, and self-ish—but they're charmed, anyway. He's not really a bad sort, just a guy with a hard-luck past and no star to guide him.

"I've gotta get someplace in this world, I just gotta," he says, his true colors showing.

Madge is crowned queen of the picnic, as expected. But she'd throw away her crown and cape for a single dance with Hal. It's remarkable how many sparks fly off that dance scene, seeing as how Holden balked at doing it and had to be paid an extra eight thousand dollars for the "stunt work." Director Joshua Logan took Holden to roadhouses and made him practice the steps over and over. No wonder the movie won an award for Best Editing. It makes Holden look like a regular Fred Astaire.

The key to the sexiness of the choreography is that the two swivel toward each other as if pulled forward by their hips, but when they finally touch hands, they pause at arm's length, as if frightened by the power of their attraction. They dance, pause, dance, pause, gradually drawing closer together. Sales of the recording "Moonglow" skyrocketed after this movie.

Madge gives herself to Hal that night after the picnic. She listens through the story of his emotionally impoverished youth. By the time he tells her of his time at the reformatory for stealing a motorcycle, she's smitten and shuts him up with a kiss. Those dangerous men and their reform-school pasts!

Madge finally makes a decision of her own, without the aid of her mother. Symbolically, her mom clings to her, trying to hold her back. But Madge has decided to follow her heart and leaves behind a town and society that tosses women away after the first blush of youth.

As luck would have it, the man with the best muscle definition for miles is the one who prizes Madge for her true self and not just her beauty.

Witness

1985

There is a world of difference between John Book and Rachel Lapp. He's a tough Philadelphia cop, a handsome loner who is not afraid to work with his hands—either to punch someone out or to build a birdhouse. She's an Amish widow, member of an old-fashioned sect that lives by strict laws regarding honesty, courtship, and how to live off the land. The two are separated by every social, cultural, and technological touchstone except for the international language of love.

"If we made love last night," he apologizes after having seen this modest widow naked at her bath, "I'd have to stay. Or you'd have to leave."

Witness is a romantic thriller that wisely keeps most of the thrills on the domestic front. Rachel's little boy (Lukas Haas) is the only witness to a cop's murder. He shows John who the killer is from a picture, on the wall of police headquarters, of a top cop (Danny Glover), which points to an inside job reaching high into the department. Soon John has been shot through the abdomen, and he whisks Rachel and her son away to Amish country, where they hole up in her farmhouse.

John's gunshot is worse than he thought. Rachel and her father-in-law get him into her bed, where Rachel tends to his wounds and fevers, applying poultices and damp cloths. Naturally, he is naked, the better to care for his body.

It is said that a woman needs to pity a man in order to love him. One could add that if she dresses his wounds, she's a goner.

There is something potently erotic about a woman dressing a man's wounds and nursing him back to health. Caretaking is a respectable, even laudable, way for a woman to have intimate contact with a man she hardly knows. She can touch his body, see him naked, handle him. It gives her permission to touch and explore. If he is half out of his mind

Even in Amish disguise, Harrison Ford is the hottest thing on Kelly McGillis's farm in the romantic thriller *Witness*.

with fever, so much the better. He will awaken with gratitude but no memory.

In movies, a wounded hero is usually wounded on the woman's behalf; he takes the bullet for her uncomplainingly. He can bear any pain as long as it is in the service of protecting a lady. And it is only fair that she minister to him uncomplainingly in return. The mighty hero is temporarily vulnerable, and the damsel in distress is temporarily in control. In movies, this Florence Nightingale display serves as an important courtship ritual.

It surely helps that John Book is played by Harrison Ford, a man's man, his body and weathered face rippling with masculine promise. Kelly McGillis plays Rachel, plain in the ways that are prized by the Amish, but with a streak of feminine defiance. When her old-fashioned father-in-law threatens that the community elders may see to it that she is shunned, she refuses to accept a sense of shame.

The movie offers a teasing hope that John can make the transition to the simplicity of Amish life. Rachel's father-in-law teaches him to milk a cow. "You never had your hands on a teat before?" he asks John in disdain. "Not one this big," he quips.

Rachel's growing attraction to John is shown in appropriately small gestures. She brings him a glass of lemonade while he is hard at work in the barn. When he drinks, some of it spills down his chin and onto his chest. She follows the rivulets with her eyes. In a society that prizes being "plain" above all else, less is more.

The movie was the first to be filmed in Pennsylvania's Lancaster County, home of the horse-and-buggy crowd, and it won two of the eight Oscars for which it was nominated (screenplay and editing). It was director Peter Weir's first American film, and he brought to it the sense of erotic mystery that prevailed in his Australian films, like *Picnic at Hanging Rock*.

The only thing Hollywood about the ending is that the bad guys get caught and justice is served. *Witness* understands that John and Rachel can never be together and proves it as early as when Rachel is tending the feverish, bullet-ridden John. He talks in his delirium. "I'll fucking kill you!" he moans. Words and sentiments like that, straight from John's wounded gut, could never be at home under an Amish roof.

At the end, John's car passes Rachel's homegrown suitor (the late Alexander Godunov) on the road. Godunov is plain enough for Rachel, even though the audience's heart is with the departing hunk.

ROLE MODELS

We can learn a lot from movies, including how to behave and who we want to be. In the following movies, the heroine is forced by circumstances beyond her control to learn the art of self-determination. In *Silence of the Lambs*, Jodie Foster rises to the challenge of her FBI assignment. In *Silkwood*, Meryl Streep's brush with radiation poisoning makes a fighter of her. In *An Unmarried Woman* and *Ms. 45*, personal disaster leads to a complete personality makeover. And in *True Lies*, Jamie Lee Curtis is a frump who spreads her wings and saves her marriage.

Zoe Tamerlis evens the score as a rape victim turned vigilante in *Ms. 45.*

Ms. 45

1981

In vigilante movie after vigilante movie, a woman's graphic defilement is used as an excuse for some guy with a death wish to go around cleaning up the town.

In *Ms. 45*, a gritty urban thriller by New York director Abel Ferrara, a woman finally avenges her own honor and manages to drain Manhattan of much of its testosterone along the way.

Frequent Ferrara colleague Zoe Tamerlis plays Thana, a naive mute girl working for a fashion designer. Mute girls often make convenient targets in exploitation movies, and this cult movie really stacks the deck.

The film is funny in a gruesome way, even though rape is a subject women don't find amusing. Thana is raped on the way home from work (the rapist is played by the director), and as if that weren't enough, she comes home to a burglary in progress in which the burglar rapes her as well. Thana is having one bitch of a day.

In the beginning of the movie, Thana is so passive, she is practically a zombie. During the second rape, she just lies there on the couch as if she has given up. There is no struggle, but her hand is within reach of a knife, and she suddenly stabs the rapist to death. It is the beginning of a new career and a new, more attractive identity.

Thana really blossoms in her new guise as vigilante. She dresses better, wears world-class makeup, and starts to look fairly foxy. It is not surprising that more men start coming on to her on the street.

But Thana is narrow in focus. She kills any man who solicits her, not just the vermin. She cuts up their bodies in the bathtub, stores the chunks in her refrigerator, and disposes of them in huge, dripping garbage bags, parceling them out to wastebaskets across the city.

Thana kills every man who is the least bit sexist. But she makes a leap of logic from there and begins to kill men regardless of their intent. Their inherent sexism is defined by their maleness. Anyone is a candidate for the .45 Thana inherited from her erstwhile burglar. Her character may be mute, but Thana's piece gives her a voice that reports volumes. By taking charge of her fate, she becomes a more interesting woman.

The set-piece ending takes place at a Halloween party, where Thana is dressed as a nun. In slow motion, she shoots every guy in the joint, except those dressed in drag.

With *Ms. 45*, director Ferrara wittily manipulates the revenge genre and shows how it ticks. The audience is so primed to hate a wimp and love an avenger that it can't help cheering the ms. despite her misfires.

Should Thana be given role-model status? Well, let's put it this way. Men cheer for Charles Bronson, Jean-Claude Van Damme, and Arnold Schwarzenegger, who take about as long to ascertain a man's villainy as Thana. Why shouldn't Zoe Tamerlis join their ranks?

Silence of the Lambs
1991

An "imago" is an insect in its final adult state, sexually mature, "typically winged," according to Webster's. In a secondary meaning, it is also an idealized mental image of the self. The imago is an important image in Jonathan Demme's *Silence of the Lambs*, about an unflappable FBI trainee (Jodie Foster) whose goal—aside from tracking the serial killer who stuffs moths down the gullets of his victims—is to achieve her own idealized mental image of the self.

Clarice Starling, the central figure of the movie, has a lot in common with the killer she's tracking. They both want to metamorphose into something grander than themselves. In Clarice's case, she is struggling to better herself and leave behind the frightened little girl with the trailer-park accent and sensible shoes. "One generation away from poor white trash" is how captive serial killer Dr. Hannibal Lecter (Anthony Hopkins) sums her up.

Lecter, a former psychiatrist known as "Hannibal the Cannibal" because he cooked and ate portions of his patients, takes a shine to Clarice because he senses her troubled past and her efforts to put all that behind her. He agrees to help her capture the killer known as Buffalo Bill by giving her cagey clues about a killer's mind and methods.

Many women skipped this five-Oscar movie because they were put off by its supposed violence. In fact, the violence is mostly hinted at. Surely the subject is on the gruesome side, but Clarice Starling is one of the strongest, most intelligent female characters ever shown on-screen. The chase is with her inner demons. Her confrontations with Lecter are all keenly intellectual. Clarice swallows her fear and pride to find a way to relate to Lecter and to draw from him the knowledge she desperately needs.

In the end, Clarice becomes the person she wants to be. She gains the respect and even affection of the craftiest serial killer on the planet. She

FBI trainee Jodie Foster learns the ropes in *The Silence of the Lambs* by using her wits—and her desire to escape her past—to catch a serial killer.

rescues an intended victim (Brooke Smith) from a pit. (Smith makes a very crafty, energetic victim.) For female viewers, *Silence of the Lambs* is not a thriller about tracking a serial killer; it's a celebration of one woman's metamorphosis.

Lecter provides Clarice with riddles and clues in return for probing deeply into her psyche to see how she ticks. One interesting aspect of the movie is that Clarice is menaced to a certain extent by every male in the film *except* Lecter, the most dangerous among them.

With point-of-view camera work, we see how Clarice sees men looking at her. They eye her suspiciously or sexually. Her boss (Scott Glenn) seems to have a veiled interest in her. Lecter's egotistical jailor (Anthony Heald) blatantly propositions her. A pack of small-town policemen at an autopsy regard her with disdain.

Only Hannibal Lecter, who is always separated from her by a wall of glass or bars, looks straight into her soul and appreciates her. "Don't lie," he warns her in his dry, genteel voice. "I'll know."

In his strangely gentlemanly way, Lecter is guaranteed never to harm Clarice, even though the end of the movie finds him escaped and on the loose.

In a scene before the escape, he reaches out from his bars and touches Clarice's hand; because he is the only male who appreciates her, that touch is the most intimate Clarice will encounter.

Silkwood

1983

Risking your life for a "moral imperative" is the sexy thing to do in *Silkwood*, a movie that sells whistle-blowing with the same subliminal message sports cars use when featuring scantily clad models in their ads. The message is that if you grow up to be like Karen Silkwood, you'll get a beefcake boyfriend like Kurt Russell.

Conspiracy theories loom large in *Silkwood*, based on the true story of an Oklahoma plutonium-plant technician who took on big business and lost her life for it. The real Karen Silkwood died in 1974 in a mysterious car crash while on her way to meet a *New York Times* reporter, presumably bringing details as to how the Kerr-McGee plant willfully neglected the safety of its employees. The plant closed down a year after Silkwood's death and eventually coughed up $10 million to her estate.

As directed by Mike Nichols from the screenplay by Nora Ephron and Alice Arlen and as played by Meryl Streep in a suitably midwestern accent, Karen is a flirtatious, hard-partying, slightly trashy assembly-line worker with no ambitions other than to finish her shift and drink beer with hunk-o-rama Drew Stephens (Russell). She has already messed up a previous live-in relationship and lost control of her three children. This careless streak endangers her relationship with Drew as well.

Karen and coworkers monitor their hands for exposure to radiation on their way in and out of the room where they toil in hospital scrubs and gloves. Every now and then employees get "cooked" from exposure to radiation. When this happens, they are scrubbed down and routinely told they are free from internal contamination, even though all the lunchroom chatter is about friends and family suffering from cancer. Everyone at Kerr-McGee smokes like a chimney, indicating how little they know or care about their own health.

Meryl Streep *(left)* turns crusader for worker safety in *Silkwood*. Lesbian subtext alert: Cher plays a roommate who secretly loves her and may have been the one who turned her in.

Karen's consciousness is raised after she gets "cooked." Thereafter she becomes active in union activities, which further alienates her from everyone, including Drew, who feels their "normal" existence slipping away. Later, her goose is really cooked. She is found to be contaminated inside and out, leaving a "hot" trail all over the house she shares with Drew and with lesbian friend Dolly (Cher). Foul play seems likely.

Both Sally Field and Jane Fonda hit it big with social-conscience movies (respectively, *Norma Rae* and *The China Syndrome*, both in 1979) a few years before. In fact, Fonda's production company owned the rights to *Silkwood* for several years. With *Silkwood*, Streep joined the ranks of this short-lived surge. Field and Jessica Lange would go on to star in, respectively, *Places in the Heart* and *Country*, both extolling farming rights, but the minigenre petered out quickly.

Streep had won an Oscar the year before for *Sophie's Choice*, so she lost this time to Shirley MacLaine for *Terms of Endearment*. Cher was also nominated but lost to Linda Hunt (*The Year of Living Dangerously*). Mike Nichols, who hadn't directed a movie in eight years, was nominated, as were the editor and screenwriters.

As for Karen Silkwood's fate, the movie floats numerous possibilities. The most likely scenario is that Karen was poisoned because of her union activities. But it also could have been the work of a spurned lover or because she witnessed a contaminated truck being broken down and buried after-hours. The infection could have come from a pinpoint hole in her glove, a hot dot thrown into her time-release allergy capsules, or from a gloved coworker innocently feeding her a piece of chewing gum. The lesbian friend who secretly loved her could have inadvertently turned her in or done so out of spite during one of their domestic spats. Whom can we trust?

Kurt Russell, that's who. Russell, in his prime at thirty-two, plays Drew as a man's man, a car mechanic and beer swiller who nevertheless is sensitive enough to kneel between Karen's thighs and tell her he wishes he could take better care of her. He does, in fact, take pretty good care of her. He cooks, fixes things, and is always up for sex. He has a broad back—most of his scenes around the house require him to be bare-chested—and a sense of humor. Karen and Drew are clearly the couple of the hour over at the plant.

For a lesbian audience, certainly the relationship between Karen and Dolly is filled with unexplored possibilities. The movie's elastic subtext hints that the promiscuous Karen indeed had something going with the lovesick Dolly. "He left because of you!" she yells at Dolly after Drew temporarily moves out.

For the rest of the female audience, it's Drew's sturdy, manly support in the background that makes Karen's risks tolerable. Yes, be a hero, get the goods on the factory bosses, become a woman with a sense of purpose, but don't neglect the boyfriend! It takes nothing away from Karen Silkwood as a model of courage and conscience to say that *Silkwood* is also, most cannily, a romance. Many a fine sports car has been sold on less.

True Lies

1994

One of the problems of the action genre, which depends on the simplicity of a black-and-white moral universe, is that female characters are given only two options: mother or whore, virtuous bore or voracious babe. Actresses are squeezed into these roles like Scarlett sucking in her breath for her corset to be tightened.

True Lies, the Arnold Schwarzenegger techno-action flick, is a rare example of the genre that attempts to bridge the gap between these sexual extremes. It reasons that if a wife can be both mother and whore at the same time — maritally faithful but sexually wild, morally upright but down and dirty — there would be no reason for a husband to stray.

And the movie does not overlook those other, more fundamental reasons why spouses cheat. It encourages married couples to find things in common and share their work life, to rely on each other in crisis, to act in tandem.

The movie's popularity among women has to do with Jamie Lee Curtis's confident and humorous performance. By playing both a mother and a whore, she is able to establish a link between the phallic universe of the action genre and the female sexuality that, as Kryptonite does to Superman, threatens to weaken and undermine it.

Schwarzenegger plays Harry Tasker, a spy whose day job is, quite literally, to save the world. At home, however, his wife Helen (Curtis) thinks he is just some computer salesman schlub. "I fall asleep in five minutes" is how Helen, a drab legal secretary, describes listening to the (phony) details of Harry's day.

Yet both Harry and Helen lead double lives. The private, exciting part of their lives they keep to themselves, while to each other they present a front of bland predictability and distinct lack of sizzle.

By the end of the movie, Harry's chief accomplishment will not be saving the world but his marriage.

Jamie Lee Curtis dresses sexy and mixes it up with the bad guys, thus becoming a better wife to Arnold Schwarzenegger in *True Lies*.

Although the movie later turns on whether Helen is cheating on Harry, it is Harry who is cheating on Helen—at least metaphorically. He is wedded to his secret life. His first line in the movie, whispered into a walkie-talkie to the backup guys in the van, is a singsong "Honey, I'm home!" This, of course, is meant to be another Arnold quotable, like "I'll be back!" or "*Hasta la vista*, baby!" But the line has greater resonance as part of an ongoing bigamy theme. His sidekick and closest buddy, Gib (Tom Arnold), drops Harry back home after their midnight tryst and reminds Harry to replace his wedding ring; Gib has been holding it for him, or, in effect, wearing it. After screwing around with global safety, Harry climbs guiltily into bed next to his comatose wife.

After a few more chases, fights, and kabooms, the real gears of the movie begin turning. Harry surprises Helen at work, only to find she's run off for lunch with a mystery suitor. While action fans may get a "takeaway" from the movie of such scenes as the causeway being blown up or Jamie Lee Curtis being hauled out of the top of an open limo and dangling from a helicopter, female audiences will more likely recall the escalating humiliations that Helen Tasker is subjected to for the bogus crime of infidelity and how Helen eventually turns these humiliations to her favor.

First, Harry spies on his wife to get the goods on the man he thinks is her lover, a sleazy used-car salesman (Bill Paxton) who pretends he's a spy(!) to get Helen excited. Harry's humiliation is played up for comic effect; in fact, however, there is no humiliation, because it turns out that the qualities Helen is attracted to are present only in her husband and not at all in the salesman. It is Harry who is the spy, Harry who is the real article, and to erase any lingering doubts, the salesman, when cornered, weeps and confesses to having a small penis. He is not a threat to Harry's masculinity.

Yet the potential of such a threat so incenses Harry that he must exact retribution. He has Helen abducted to a chillingly bare interrogation room, where, from behind a one-way mirror, he and Gib, their voices electronically altered, harangue her with increasingly personal questions.

Now Harry's plan is to forcibly release the wild woman that quivers beneath Helen's skin. He gives her a fake spying assignment that requires her to pose as a prostitute. Awkwardly, and then with increasing expertise, she performs an erotic dance of a very particular, commercial type—the kind that is only found at topless clubs. Since Helen Tasker isn't the kind of woman who would have frequented such joints, it is implied that the standard gyrations of the topless club are innate in every woman, as innate as, say, motherhood is thought to be. At last, the biological link between the mother and the whore that every sexually tormented male has been looking for!

The movie's idea is to rehabilitate Helen first as a wife and then as a woman. Once Helen is certified virginal (i.e., faithful to her husband) through interrogation, the plan is to make her sexually palatable again within the confines of marriage by turning her into Harry's personal whore. He is the mystery figure who sits in the chair in the dark of the hotel room and approvingly observes those bumps and grinds, meant just for him.

Now Helen is a perfect wife, both saintly and sexual. But there still remains the problem of outside interference. Tia Carrerre plays a single career woman and as such is the greatest threat to the Tasker marriage. Just like the Glenn Close character in *Fatal Attraction*, the single career woman is unstable, suspect, and must be dispatched by her married rival. In this case, Helen scratches the woman's face with her wedding ring.

Action movies are often, maybe always, about the hero's phallic power. Fortunately, writer-director James Cameron has a history of including strong-willed heroines who provide titillation for male viewers and powerful figures of identification for female viewers. They are usually pumped up, braless, humorless, and wear tank tops into combat. In *True Lies*, Helen has something extra—a sense of humor. When she dances erotically, she falls over and bounds back. Helen is able to fulfill Harry's fantasies without really buying into them, something most women have already secretly learned how to do.

An Unmarried Woman

1978

When you think of the guy leaving the girl, you think of Rhett walking off just as Scarlett was finally realizing what she was losing. And you know that in some parallel universe, even though the movie is over, Scarlett is working her bustle off to get him back.

It would be nearly forty years before a man would leave a woman, where it would not only be the best thing that ever happened to her, but she'd have her own chance to turn down the Rhett du jour. *An Unmarried Woman* screams the message "My body, my choice!"

In that parallel universe, of course, Jill Clayburgh was probably establishing just enough independence that her personhood would not be all that adversely affected by marrying the sweetly bear-like Alan Bates. In a movie that is acerbic about everything from cheating husbands to the singles scene, Alan Bates plays a pure Prince Charming of the SoHo set.

It was only the timing of the movie in take-no-prisoners 1978 that allowed an unmarried woman to walk away from such a prime catch. Paul Mazursky's divorce comedy came out at the height of feminist consciousness raising, when women were more excited by female bonding and personal growth than by being impaled on a white picket fence in the suburbs. *An Unmarried Woman* was the feminist primer of the day, showing what it was like to go through the emotional crisis of divorce, to be in therapy, to jump back in the dating pool, to be a single mom.

The postdivorce healing process may sound like drudgery. But not when Clayburgh is at the center of it in her panties and cotton T-shirt, dancing *Swan Lake* through her swank Upper East Side apartment at the beginning of the movie and then plowing steadily uptown with Bates's painting as her sail at the end of the movie.

Clayburgh plays Erica, whose spineless husband (Michael Murphy)

Alan Bates is the sexiest painter in SoHo, but Jill Clayburgh has learned to make it on her own in *An Unmarried Woman*.

breaks down in tears in the street and confesses he's in love with another woman. In fact, he's been seeing her for a year. With this news, Erica's world collapses and turns bilious—and it was quite striking to see a well-known actress vomit in the middle of West Broadway.

Erica finds she must not only get over her fifteen-year marriage; she also must redefine herself from the ground up. She goes into therapy, where her shrink is played by Mazursky's real-life shrink, Penelope Russianoff. The idea was to lend the psychiatric sessions an air of reality, although Russianoff is as scary a shrink as you'll find.

Erica finally screws up her courage to go on a date, and the whole depressing singles scene is summed up by her skeevy one-night stand with Cliff Gorman.

Finally, Erica meets Saul (Bates), a handsome, cuddly British painter. A single woman couldn't ask for better. "Underneath this haunted, driven shell of a man," begs Saul, "lives a warm homebody who likes to watch TV and chew cashews while the woman he loves is finishing a good novel."

"Sounds like my marriage," quips Erica.

The movie was a huge hit and received three Oscar nominations. Today it is a footnote, as is Clayburgh's once promising career. For a brief, shining moment, it was the great hope of women that it would pave the way for female-centered movies, featuring actresses of a certain maturity who could have so many riches at their feet that they even had the luxury of turning down Alan Bates.

IMPOSSIBLE LOVE

Who said only men were interested in the chase? The rule of thumb is that the more impossible the love, the more satisfying the movie; once you get into "happily ever after" territory, the drama peters out. Plus, women have a stake in seeing affairs end badly; in real life, so many of them do, but not nearly so nobly as in *Back Street* or *Waterloo Bridge*. Celia Johnson awakens from her *Brief Encounter* as from a dream. Montgomery Clift's background and bad behavior make it impossible for Elizabeth Taylor to keep him in *A Place in the Sun*. And Gene Tierney cannot consummate her passion for Rex Harrison in *The Ghost and Mrs. Muir* unless she crosses into another dimension.

Fannie Hurst's novel about a doomed love affair with a married man proved to be such a popular theme that *Back Street* was made three times. In 1932, Irene Dunne sacrificed personal happiness to remain true to John Boles. (Courtesy of Photofest)

Back Street

1932, 1941, 1961

The nobility of obsession is raised to ludicrous heights in *Back Street*, in which the Other Woman endures the life of a doormat for the married man to whom she is devoted. "When you love somebody, that's it" is Susan Hayward's uncontested philosophy in the 1961 version.

Even though the heroine's self-abasement is a little rough on today's women, they continue to rent this old chestnut from the video stores. "Am I late?" her boyfriends always ask. "I was early!" she chirps.

And to the lover who over the years can never manage to get a divorce: "You know I'll be there, wherever you are, whenever you say. . . . My life is rich and wonderful, loving you and being loved by you."

In the three versions of *Back Street*, the back-street woman becomes successively more career oriented, to the point where 1961's Hayward is an internationally successful dress designer. The career does no good for strengthening her spine, but it serves to explain her mobility in following John Gavin around Europe as he tends to his own business.

For those susceptible to tears — and who in the audience is not? — it is not Gavin's death that's the hard thing to take. (His orphaned children seem to become Hayward's by default.) The tearjerker is the excruciatingly painful scene in which the wedding dress Hayward designed and will obviously never wear is auctioned off to her lover's haughty wife (Vera Miles).

In the earlier versions, all based on the Fannie Hurst novel, Irene Dunne and Margaret Sullavan played the back-street lover to John Boles and Charles Boyer, respectively. The 1941 version is the most effective, with the lovers thwarted at first by circumstance and thereafter by their own bad judgment. At the end, they both die and are united, presumably in some front-street love nest in heaven. In the 1961 version the married man and his wife die, leaving Hayward the rather odd comfort of being

In the 1941 and 1961 remakes, Margaret Sullavan and Susan Hayward sacrificed personal happiness to remain true to Charles Boyer and John Gavin, respectively. (Courtesy of Photofest)

de facto mother to her lover's children. In fact, this not very legally plausible ending is part of the mean enjoyment of the movie. The wife taunts Hayward about never getting to wear her wedding dress, but Hayward has had the husband and now gets the kids, and therefore the last laugh. (Catfight alert!)

Back Street is a weepie by design. Helping it along is the classic plight of the Other Woman, she who spends holidays alone, who is beset by doubts about her loyalty to her lover, who must take a backseat in addition to living on a back street, whose time and energies are at the mercy of a man who, every day, is breaking his vows to another. Doting on a married man offers few rewards. "What do you have? Waiting? Worrying?" asks Gavin. "Loving you and knowing you love me," replies Hayward. "Oh, Paul, I have all that!"

Back Street makes a furious case for the nobility of suffering, for the painful satisfaction of romantic obsession. It's a tough case to make, but so many sufferers, having tried all else (except a twelve-step program), need that sugar pill. Impossible love has its masochistic rewards.

Brief Encounter
1945

The exquisite torture of illicit love is burned onto the screen—with the help of a lot of Rachmaninoff—in *Brief Encounter*, the story of two ordinary married people in love. The problem is that they are not married to each other.

"It can't last—this misery can't last," Laura Jesson reassures herself. "Not even life lasts very long."

Oscar-nominated Celia Johnson plays Laura, a sensible middle-aged Englishwoman who spends her Thursdays shopping and taking in a matinee. Then she has a spot of tea at the railway station before her train takes her home to husband and children.

One evening on the train platform, she gets a mote of dust in her eye, which must explain why her judgment becomes temporarily clouded. Is there a doctor in the house? There is indeed, in the form of general practitioner Alec Harvey (Trevor Howard). For the next few Thursdays, they meet, spend the day, have a few laughs, fall madly in love.

This love is doomed, which we know because of the graceful opening scene in which the two sit at the cafe waiting for their trains and communicating without many words just how desperate their parting is. Their last moments together are interrupted by an old biddy who recognizes Laura and plants herself at the lovers' table. When Alec's train arrives, he places a hand meaningfully on Laura's shoulder, and then he's outta there.

It is only once Laura gets home that she starts to tell us, via voice-over narration and flashback, about her brief encounter with a married man. She tells the story as if she were confessing all to her husband, who sits by, blissfully unaware, working on his crossword puzzle. We're a happily married couple, she thinks to herself. And I must never forget that.

In flashback we see how it all started—innocently enough. "I'm an

Celia Johnson and Trevor Howard, married to others, are riding a rowboat to nowhere as they begin their brief encounter.

ordinary woman!" Laura marvels, as if this "love" thing couldn't possibly happen to someone like her. "We must be sensible!" is her rallying cry.

She is indeed ordinary, and so is her new friend. These are middle-aged people for whom passion is a degrading and uncomfortable emotion. Their one serious attempt to consummate their relationship ends abruptly when the man who owns the apartment to which they've retreated comes home unexpectedly. Now they feel cheap! Tawdry!

Brief Encounter is the *Bridges of Madison County* of its time, a housewife's daydream, a flirtation that raises the spirits without, in this case, technically breaking any vows. Laura comes close to killing herself over her lost love; he's off to practice medicine in Africa, and he's taking his family. She finds herself safe back home, no real harm done.

And it turns out that her husband has guessed it all. "Laura, whatever your dream was, it wasn't a very happy one, was it?" he murmurs to her. "You've been a long way away. Thank you for coming back to me."

Noël Coward helped adapt his play *Still Life* to make *Brief Encounter*, which explains its wonderfully nuanced script. When Laura's husband is looking for a seven-letter word for his crossword puzzle, she supplies it. "Romance. Yes, I think it's romance." Yes, it is romance of the highest order.

David Lean's direction underscores the hopeless nature of the affair by the dramatic comings and goings of the trains in the station. And there's that Rachmaninoff theme music—the *Second Piano Concerto*—which would be even more effective if it hadn't been appropriated for the sappy pop tune "All by Myself."

Once again, romance is directly proportional to the impossibility of the situation. Because Laura winds up risking nothing except her emotions, *Brief Encounter* is safe. And in a humdrum life, shattered emotions are a welcome thing, a sign of having loved and lost, proof that there is more to this ordinary, middle-aged housewife than meets the eye. It's the perfect infidelity daydream for another boring afternoon.

The Ghost and Mrs. Muir

1947

On the silver screen, lovers can cross cultural zones, overcome language barriers and parental disapproval, and defy all odds. But the ghost and Mrs. Muir truly inhabit different worlds, the dead and the living, and never the twain shall meet.

The newly widowed Lucy Muir (Gene Tierney), with her daughter (Natalie Wood) in tow, buys a remote, windswept cottage by the sea. She buys it cheap because no one else wants it; it is said to be haunted by the former owner, sea captain Daniel Gregg (Rex Harrison). The captain's stern portrait stares down potential buyers.

But Lucy isn't scared off so easily. The captain must go to excessive lengths to try to rid his hideaway of these new pests. Moans and gusts of wind have no effect, so finally he does his worst. He reveals himself to her. Why, shiver me timbers, it's Rex Harrison! No wonder Lucy Muir isn't going anyplace in a hurry!

Captain Gregg is dashing, irascible, moody, tempestuous, funny—everything you'd want in a live-in companion. He cares for her, too. When Lucy needs money to keep up payments on the house, the captain dictates his salty memoirs, and Lucy sells them under her name to a publisher. The two couldn't be more intimate if they were lovers.

Which, in a sense, they are. Certainly they are in love. They live together, work together, and are powerfully affected by each other. The force of this romance comes from the central conundrum: The lovers can never truly be lovers. They cannot touch, kiss, cuddle, or have sex. A ghost can't even take cold showers, although certainly he can watch his human counterpart take one. (The captain can hide himself at will.)

The humor of their situation was mined in the television series of the same name in the late 1960s. There is a long tradition of ghosts in movies.

Rex Harrison's salty charms soon have widow Gene Tierney in thrall to him in *The Ghost and Mrs. Muir*. Too bad he's already dead.

They were first used as comic devices. Actors with bedsheets over their heads wreaked havoc among the living as far back as the silents. Later, ghosts became scary, even kitschy.

But the 1947 movie version is neither funny nor scary. Instead, it is a classic weepie, which is the main indicator of a gratifying movie to many a woman. The captain ends up making the most enormous sacrifice he can for the woman he loves: He makes himself invisible to her for the rest of her life so as to encourage her to lead a normal, human existence with men of flesh.

Unfortunately, the men of flesh don't work out, as men of flesh are wont to do. George Sanders courts Lucy, but he's just another married man having his little fun. Lucy sours on men and spends the rest of her days alone in that cottage.

Only when she is very, very old and feeble and dies in her favorite chair, looking out toward the captain's beloved sea, does Rex Harrison step forward from the shadows to take her with him into the afterlife. There, presumably, they will be joined in the same spirit world. Bring on the waterworks!

The Ghost and Mrs. Muir affirms many treasured beliefs for women. One is that love is a bond so strong, it can weather the setback of death; eternal love knows no bounds. The dead will wait for us. Even better, they'll hang around, restless spirits with unfinished business that they are, to see us through our days. Believing in ghosts is a way of holding on to loved ones just a little longer. They are like an angel on the shoulder.

Another consolation of the movie is its proof of an afterlife, one of the most seductive existential concepts.

There is yet another advantage of imagining a ghostly lover for oneself. There is a purity in such a love. The lonely widow couldn't very well be sharing a house with an unmarried man, not in 1947, but this man's otherworldliness makes such intimacy safe. If Lucy can't have him right then and there, at least this ghost is such a fine figure of a man that he's worth waiting a lifetime for.

A Place in the Sun

1951

The smoldering scenes between Montgomery Clift and Elizabeth Taylor make *A Place in the Sun* one of those unforgettable romances. Knowing what we know about the actors' offscreen lives puts even more of a spin on the theme of impossible love.

In the movie, based on the Theodore Dreiser novel *An American Tragedy*, Clift plays an earnest social climber who works his way up in his rich uncle's bathing-suit factory from assembly-line worker to production manager. As he starts making it big, he earns an entrée to the fabulous world of rich, beautiful people, one that includes socialite Elizabeth Taylor.

"I see you had a misspent youth," she says when she first sees him doing a trick shot at the pool table. But it wasn't a misspent youth so much as lower-class one, with no money and little education.

When he finds out that Taylor is in love with him, Clift sees all possibilities opening before him. And they would have except for that little matter of Shelley Winters, the coarse, petulant factory girl who is pregnant with his child. She commands him to marry her, which would deprive him forever of a place in the sun. He dreams of drowning her in the lake.

She does, in fact, drown in the lake. In the movie, it's an accident, and he gets the electric chair, anyway. In real life—this incident was based on a true story—an heir to the Gillette razor fortune really did hit the girl with an oar and sink her, then had the temerity to sell signed photos of himself from death row.

It's easy to feel compassionate for Clift's character. He yearns to make something of himself, and Clift makes this hunger so desperate and pathetic that women want to mother him. "Tell Mama," says Taylor the first time they kiss. "Tell Mama all."

He doesn't quite fit with the "in" crowd, but Montgomery Clift tries to find a place in the sun with a receptive Elizabeth Taylor, both on and off the screen.

And who can blame such a man for falling in love with seventeen-year-old Elizabeth Taylor?

Taylor's allure is such that even Clift, a gay man, had a fling with her during the making of the movie. Taylor mooned incessantly over her costar, sending him love letters that Clift passed on to his boyfriends, according to C. David Heymann's biography *Liz*. The two became good friends and even attempted to have sex—unsuccessfully at first, but with better luck much later. Clift would sit in the bathroom with Taylor and run lines with her as she bathed three times daily.

Clift was largely compassionate toward Liz, even though he refused most of her sexual entreaties and, according to Heymann, got the teenager hooked on Benzedrine as a pick-me-up during their hectic shooting schedule.

Meanwhile, director George Stevens hated Taylor. He thought she was exactly like the character she was playing—a spoiled, insulated rich girl who knew nothing of real life. Stevens tortured Taylor in the icy water of autumnal Lake Tahoe, where they were shooting as if it were summer. "George [Stevens] sat in a boat with his big boots on and his earmuffs and gloves and made us do take after take after take," said Taylor later. "I wanted to kill him." In character or out, Taylor faced the disapproval of her "father" and her director and was in love with a man she just couldn't have—which, for movie purposes, is the most emotionally satisfying kind of love there is.

What was behind the scenes, then, mirrored what was on celluloid. Even the movie's love rivals didn't get along: Taylor and Winters were worlds apart and hated each other. The audience can feel the honesty of what they're seeing, which is probably why the movie won six of the nine Oscars for which it was nominated.

Waterloo Bridge
1940

Myra Lester and Capt. Roy Cronin "meet cute" on Waterloo Bridge during a World War I air raid. She drops the contents of her purse, he helps her pick it up. While making small talk in the bomb shelter, she tells him she's a ballerina. "Must be good for the muscles of the . . ." he fumbles.

Indeed, those mysterious muscles are in fine form. So is her face. Myra is played by Vivien Leigh, her first role since *Gone With the Wind*, which made her the hottest property this side of Tara. With her luminous beauty and mischievous smile, you'd never know Leigh was furious that new hubby Laurence Olivier didn't get the Robert Taylor part of the dashing captain. (Olivier went off to make *Pride and Prejudice*; both of them needed a cash infusion after their respective divorces.)

Myra and Cronin fall in love. But the good captain is called away to battle just hours before they are to be married. Myra waits faithfully, but the money dwindles, especially since she and her girlfriend Kitty (Virginia Field) have been fired from their production of *Swan Lake* by the battle-ax ballet mistress Madame Olga (scary Maria Ouspenskaya).

After reading in the papers of Cronin's disappearance, Myra gives up her captain for dead. She turns to the only kind of career for a looker — hooker.

One day, while Myra is trolling for johns at Waterloo Station, Cronin turns up, none the worse for having been a prisoner of war. "Darling, don't cry," he implores. "It's a happy ending!"

But there are no happy endings in *Waterloo Bridge* or in most old movies where the heroine isn't virginal.

Reputation is everything in the captain's aristocratic world. He makes that clear to Myra right from the start, when he leaves her in the car so he can get clearance to marry from his commanding officer. For this, he needs Myra's "vital statistics," the social equivalent of running a credit check.

By becoming a prostitute in the interim, Myra has ensured that she

93

War is indeed hell for Vivien Leigh in *Waterloo Bridge*
when she finds that her love for Robert Taylor doesn't
put as much food on the table as trolling the train
station for johns.

can never marry "up." She tries, anyway, since Cronin is too dense to
figure out how Myra's been supporting herself in his absence. But she
knows that one day the truth will out and she will have met her Waterloo. So she does the only respectable thing under the circumstances: She
leaves Cronin without telling him why and throws herself under the
wheels of an oncoming military truck on the bridge where they met.

Impossible love is always a heartbreak. What makes *Waterloo Bridge*
even tougher to bear—and therefore more satisfying—is that Myra really
did have other choices. She came within a hair's breadth of having everything she wanted in life, but she blew it at every turn.

Shall we make a list? Myra could have kept her job if she hadn't gone to see her soldier off on the train. (As it was, she hardly made it in time to wave from the platform.) She could have prevailed upon Cronin's accommodating mother for help. Hell, Myra could have sold her bouquet of freshly delivered flowers for a hot meal if she hadn't had such a sentimental attachment to them. She could have gotten a less respectable music-hall job that would have kept those muscles of the you-know-what in good shape without compromising them. Leaving Cronin for the good of his name was a noble act, but this was only after a series of poor judgments.

Under the rubric of a romance that was fated not to be lies the familiar story of a woman who constantly shoots herself in the foot. Myra's self-destructive urges doom her to a life of missed moments. One could argue that she became a prostitute because she was poor and desperate, but that is not entirely the case. The first time she accepts a strange man's invitation is because she feels hopeless, abandoned, and pathetic. It happens while she is standing on the bridge where she first met the love of her life, when she is feeling particularly sorry for herself. Like the woman who seduces her lover's best friend during some snit, one impetuous act of self-loathing can make it impossible ever to set things right again.

Meanwhile, Myra's friend Kitty takes to the oldest profession for a much healthier reason; she does it because she needs the money to care for the heartsick Myra. Kitty loses her ballet job for Myra, quitting in protest as a show of solidarity. She continues to stick by Myra through thick and thin. (Is there another story here?) By comparison, Myra skips off the minute her captain returns, leaving Kitty in her own litter.

It's not any fun to be the sort of person who continually screws things up by acting out. (If only Myra had controlled herself during her initial lunch with Mrs. Cronin, the old lady wouldn't have thought Myra so bizarre.) That is why Myra, as played by the glamorous Leigh, is so treasured a character—a beautiful, misunderstood woman who should not be judged by her mistakes but by the pureness within.

Years later, Cronin—now a colonel on his way to yet another world war—pauses on Waterloo Bridge to reminisce. Women who fear they lost someone because of their own stupid blunders will be happy to believe that those men can never forget them, that the guys' lives will be meaningless and their hearts hollow all of their days.

FUNNY GIRLS

If women got a nickel for every time they were told they had no sense of humor when they didn't laugh at jokes made at their expense, they'd be able to finance more movies like these. Holly Hunter is a lovable neurotic TV producer in *Broadcast News*; Alicia Silverstone proves that an airhead teen can learn a trick or two in *Clueless*; Goldie Hawn brings her electric toothbrush to basic training in *Private Benjamin*. *Mrs. Parker and the Vicious Circle* is a tragedy about the twentieth century's funniest woman. And the underrated *Soapdish* is brimming with funny female performances.

This is the closest frustrated professional Holly Hunter gets to having sex in *Broadcast News*—speaking into William Hurt's ear to guide him through a live newscast.

Broadcast News

1987

People in the media love to roll in their own mud. James L. Brooks, a successful sitcom creator before he began directing movies, filled his *Broadcast News* with all sorts of in-jokes about "the business,"such as Holly Hunter's need to read all the papers every day, no matter what town she's on location in. As a child, her character already has a copy editor's anal-retentive interest in detail.

In our media-savvy society, these jokes don't go over anyone's head. *Broadcast News* turned out to be a slick, accessible satire of the television news business, about how natural selection chooses style over substance.

For women, *Broadcast News* was a revelation, a movie at whose center was an ambitious, neurotic, smart, lovable woman who struggles without a road map to juggle love and career. She's good at what she does, and she tolerates her own frailties. And she's adorably funny, even when she doesn't mean to be.

Jane Craig (Holly Hunter), like the other characters in the movie, has found a career compatible with her childhood personality. She's high-strung, obsessive, and principled; therefore, she becomes a TV news producer on a personal mission to retain quality news gathering in an age of sound bites.

Her colleagues, Aaron Altman (Albert Brooks) and Tom Grunick (William Hurt), are also in the business because their early personalities steered them that way. Aaron is a wordsmith, the kind who, when cornered in the schoolyard, taunted the bullies with harsh truths. In return, the bullies would beat him up. As an adult, Aaron still takes the punches, speaking truth in an industry that slathers on the varnish. Because of this, Aaron will never make it big, nor will he ever win Jane as anything more than a good friend. His plea that neediness should be considered a turn-on is one of the movie's classic funny lines.

Tom, on the other hand, is fully aware that he's not all that bright. He relies instead on charm to win people over. He makes a nice presentation. He may not be a real newsman, but he has people like Jane around to make him look good.

Aaron loves Jane, and Jane is dazzled by Tom, proving exactly what Jane hates—that the public goes for beauty over truth, for entertainment over news. Tom represents everything she despises. He's vacuous, untrained, and unworthy. And she has the hots for him.

The producer's life is so hectic that Jane schedules into her day a quiet time in which to cry out all her frustrations. She knows she has sacrificed a love life for her career, but hope springs eternal. When Tom is her date for an industry dinner, she fusses over what to wear and makes a show of walking into a shower of cologne droplets, like a high schooler on a first date.

But Tom and Jane never wind up getting together. The closest they come to sex is when she coaches him through a live newscast via an earpiece. He is excited by the rhythm and timing of her voice in his ear, and he pounces on her after the show in postcoital bliss, rolling her back and forth in her swivel chair. "I want to know what it's like to be inside you!" he says, to her horror.

Instinct finally takes over, and Jane and Tom plan a weekend getaway. In a last-minute airport showdown, Jane's conscience bounces back. Not even a weekend of hot sex can deter her from her principles. And so the heroine does something rare in the movies: She gives up the cute guy, who is not such a bad sort, after all, and holds out for something better.

A tacked-on ending lets us know that she does wind up with a nice boyfriend (unseen), although it is clear that she's still struggling with the demons of independence and intimacy. An honest ending, even if not traditionally satisfying.

Clueless
1995

Alicia Silverstone learns that " 'tis a far far better thing doing stuff for other people" in *Clueless*, a sweet-natured movie that somehow manages to bring back the lovable airhead of decades past without making feminists blanch.

Despite its much-touted but tenuous relationship to Jane Austen's novel *Emma*, *Clueless* is set in the mall world of today's Beverly Hills, where high school senior Cher (Silverstone) blithely narrates her own coming of age.

"Dionne is my friend because we both know what it's like to have people be jealous of us," Cher says in voice-over as she welcomes us to her world of privilege and microconcerns. "Dionne and I were both named after great singers of the past who now do infomercials."

Her mom died "in a freak accident during a routine liposuction," leaving Cher alone with her lawyer dad (Dan Hedaya) and a distantly related by marriage brother, Josh (Paul Rudd), who is cute and college-age. Josh has come to visit for the holidays, which distresses Cher. As a point of comparison, Josh reads Nietzsche by the pool, while all Cher knows about Hamlet she got from the Mel Gibson movie.

Cher is "a total Betty," to use her own parlance, who coordinates the day's outfits by computer matching. She has strict rules about whom she hangs out with at school, based on social status and fashion sense. Her oral report for teacher Wallace Shawn on the Haitian boat people compares them to dinner-party guests who neglect to RSVP. She has initiative enough to challenge bad grades but no appreciation of the essence of things.

Her father adores her but worries that she's not applying herself. "What did you do at school today?" he asks. She purses her mouth in a crooked line that indicates heavy thought and replies: "Well, I broke in my purple clogs."

Alicia Silverstone takes another opportunity at school to break in her purple clogs in *Clueless*, in which she plays a Beverly Hills rich kid dabbling in noblesse oblige.

Cher acts only out of self-interest, but she finds that doing makeovers on mousy teachers and collecting used ski equipment for earthquake-ravaged desert countries have rewards beyond the better grades she was initially aiming for. "*Project!*" she squeals when she befriends a hopeless new girl at school and decides to make her a total Betty.

"I had to give myself snaps for all the good deeds I was doing," she says in voice-over.

The crisis that precipitates a reevaluation of her priorities is when the "total Betty" she created goes after her brother. Cher realizes that *she* loves Josh. (The movie takes great pains to emphasize that he's not *really* her brother; he's the son of her father's former wife.)

To be loved by Josh, Cher realizes she'd have to be a more serious person, one who doesn't switch from CNN to the twenty-four-hour cartoon station. Can Cher do a makeover on herself?

When women are depicted as stupid on-screen, it's usually as bimbos who serve as window dressing or objects of derision. Cher, on the other hand, is willfully ignorant, not stupid. When boys leer at her, she rolls her eyes and utters her trademark "As if!" Even if her motivation is selfish, her little "projects" and makeovers yield beneficial results. By the end of the movie, she is actually making sense in her current-events class.

The pressure to provide movies with tough, smart heroines can come across on-screen as an exhausting obligation. A character like Cher is a relief—precious and amusing. She won't destroy the strides women have made by being mistaken for a role model. As if!

Mrs. Parker and the Vicious Circle
1995

In the 1920s and 1930s, Dorothy Parker and her literati pals were famous for their bon mots, tossed back with a few too many cocktails over a round table in the Algonquin Hotel restaurant. Parker and the gentle humorist Robert Benchley were particularly close. When Dorothy, or "Mrs. Parker," as he referred to her, was fired from her magazine job, he quit in sympathy. He was always there for her, including after her failed marriages and attempted suicides.

When a visitor spied Mrs. Parker and Mr. Benchley having a tête-à-tête in Central Park, she asked someone, "Would that be Mrs. Benchley?" And he replied, "That *would* be Mrs. Benchley if there were not already a Mrs. Benchley."

Now *there's* an American tragedy. At one time our premier wit—certainly the sharpest when it came to human foibles, her own included—Dorothy Parker led an increasingly miserable existence, fueled by booze, bitterness, and failed relationships. She deserved better. She deserved Robert Benchley, the only man who unfailingly loved her for herself.

"Why have we never misbehaved?" Mrs. Parker asks him finally in *Mrs. Parker and the Vicious Circle.*

The movie never gives a satisfactory answer, since there is no real answer now that both are dead and buried. Benchley was married, a teetotaler, and a man of gentility—at least during the early Algonquin days. Later, he became a drunk and received much of his inspiration from life at a bordello.

Jennifer Jason Leigh plays the pioneering, self-destructive writer. The actress studied audiotapes of Parker reciting her poetry to get the laconic, upper-crust voice right. She studied so well that initial test audiences couldn't understand a thing she was saying, and much of the dialogue had to be relooped.

Jennifer Jason Leigh and Campbell Scott never consummate their passion for each other in *Mrs. Parker and the Vicious Circle*, based on the miserable love life of the funniest woman of the twentieth century. (Courtesy of Photofest)

Campbell Scott, son of Colleen Dewhurst and George C. Scott, plays Benchley. Although he looks nothing like the portly gent, Scott gets the self-effacing body language down pat.

Dorothy Parker had a slim output during her lifetime despite her out-sized talent. She is the mascot for many a lugubrious female college student, representing the ideal of the suffering artist, water everywhere and not a drop to drink. Her sexual trysts become increasingly short and desperate as she becomes more a symbol of fame than flesh and blood.

It is easy—and romantic—to think of Benchley as the one man who could have saved Dorothy from herself. It's important for lovers of the downward spiral to believe that help is near at hand if only the sufferer can see past her puffy eyes.

With what we know of our doomed heroine (who managed to out-live her entire circle), could Robert Benchley really have made a difference? He was much too nice to her to be her "type." Who's to say she wouldn't have sabotaged this relationship the way she had so many others?

Ah, but the romance of it all—the smart-set writer in an unholy fascination with the possibilities of being Mrs. Benchley, if only there were not already a Mrs. Benchley. Parker looks upon the real Mrs. B. (Jennifer Beals) with both envy and repulsion. The missus represents a life of suburban domestic bliss that all women are brought up to expect (or at least consider an option). Mrs. Benchley is a good mother, a patient wife, an immaculate housekeeper. To Mrs. Parker, this woman is an alien from outer space. Dorothy Parker could never have traded in her career and independence for such a life, even though she never fulfilled her promise as a writer, either. This movie is for fans of the between-a-rock-and-a-hard-place school of romantic suffering.

Private Benjamin
1980

"I've never not belonged to someone," mourns Judy Benjamin in *Private Benjamin*, a comedy of self-affirmation. As her own father puts it after hubby number two dies of a heart attack during wedding-night sex, "She's twenty-eight years old and trained to do nothing."

Judy, played by Goldie Hawn, is a woman who defines herself by the men in her life. Her resulting self-absorption has become so focused that her biggest crisis is whether the upholsterer can match the piping on the ottoman to the mushroom color she's picked out for the study.

A widow at twenty-eight, with no prospects, she gets suckered by a recruiter into joining the army. "It'll be like three years at LaCosta!" she exclaims when told they'll get her into shape.

Her first day of basic training is a disaster. "Is green the only color these come in?" she demands of her regulation-issue khakis. "There must be some mistake. Yes, I joined the Army, but I joined the one with the condos and the private rooms."

She makes an immediate enemy of her immediate superior (Eileen Brennan, who, along with Hawn, was nominated for an Oscar) and winds up scrubbing the latrine with her electric toothbrush.

During war games, she learns map skills. ("What am I, Magellan?") During parachute drill, she learns to jump fearlessly when it's a choice between that or sex with the gung-ho colonel. The Army makes a woman of her, so much so that she experiences real orgasms for the first time. She saunters into a bar in uniform, picks up French gynecologist Armand Assante, demurs only until she finds out he is Jewish, then has great sex: "Now I know what I've been faking all these years."

By the end of the movie, Private Benjamin is her own woman, defined

Goldie Hawn is more a princess than a private until the army makes a new woman of her in *Private Benjamin*.

by her own aspirations and desires. She tosses her wedding veil and lets it float off into the air.

For a brief time in the early 1980s former *Laugh-In* bimbo Goldie Hawn was considered a major force in Hollywood, one of the few women who might have turned the male-dominated industry around to a woman's perspective.

It wasn't to be. But she did facilitate the making of *Private Benjamin*, a box-office hit about a Jewish-American princess who gets a little dirt under her fingernails. Hawn executive-produced and starred in the movie, and it remains a fine example of the stillborn genre of feminist comedy.

Coming two years after *An Unmarried Woman*, *Private Benjamin* was, in its way, both a spoof and a remake. "I didn't get it," Judy complains to a girlfriend about the Jill Clayburgh movie. "I'd be Mrs. Alan Bates in a second!"

When Judy has a chance at Armand Assante, the poor man's Alan Bates, she, too, decides to take a walk. Now she gets it.

There is even homage paid to the vomit scene of *An Unmarried Woman*. Judy isn't allowed out of an exhausting military exercise unless she collapses or throws up. Experienced bulimic that she is, she puts a finger down her throat.

Soapdish

1991

"I realize I'm not a young woman," seethes Celeste Talbert, imperious diva of the daytime soap opera *The Sun Also Sets*. "However, could you please point out to our new costume designer that I don't feel quite right in a *turban*! What I feel like is Gloria fucking Swanson!"

Sally Field is really funny—and, yes, we really like her—in the underrated comedy *Soapdish*, about how truth is stranger than the fiction of daytime TV. While not consistently funny, the movie is a stellar showcase of women in large and small roles, including Whoopi Goldberg as the show's head writer, Carrie Fisher as a casting-couch casting director, Cathy Moriarty as a scheming bit player, Kathy Najimy as a well-meaning costumer ("I thought maybe we could try the Tammy Faye Baker look"), and Teri Hatcher as a pneumatic second banana.

Field plays Celeste, an aging soap sweetheart who, offstage, is a frustrated bitch ("the queen of misery," as programming director Garry Marshall calls her). Each year, she wins another statuette for her various jail and deathbed scenes and thanks her supporting cast, "who give a new meaning to the word supporting." The camera cuts to three of those supporters, who behind their fixed smiles and appropriately teary eyes mutter under their breath: "Bitch!" "Hag!" "I hate her so much!"

It's a dog-eat-dog world on the set of this overheated show. Scheming and backstabbing are as common as the show's scripted love triangles and brain tumors. Celeste has devoted her life to the show and in return gets plot lines that explore, as the show's producer puts it, issues that concern Celeste personally: "today's woman as she gets dried up, old, and sexually undesirable."

In addition to addressing the concerns of aging career women in a comic way, there is a wealth of fine female supporting roles, giving, as

109

"I'm too young for a turban!" wails soap-opera diva Sally Field to concerned series writer Whoopi Goldberg in the comedy *Soapdish*, filled with hilarious female performances.

Celeste might say, new meaning to the phrase. Carrie Fisher is shown auditioning the well-defined Costas Mandylor for a bit part as a waiter taking someone's order. "Hmm, I don't know, try one without your shirt," she suggests.

Soapdish was the second in a series of three movies (*Ghost; The Player*) in which Whoopi Goldberg rejuvenated her career by playing understated comic supporting roles. As head writer of *The Sun Also Sets*, she must explain to the show's director why he can't bring Kevin Kline back into the story line. "He died twenty years ago in a car accident," she says with just a slight edge of irritation. "He was decapitated. The man has no head. I can't write dialogue for a man with no head."

Field, an actress whose exuberance can certainly be annoying at times, is funnier here than she has ever been. For all the self-righteous characters she has played (the union dynamo in *Norma Rae*, the avenging mother in *An Eye for an Eye*), she displays expert comic skill and timing. It's a gem of a performance that touches women in places in the heart.

SCHOOLGIRL CRUSHES

The first time a young girl feels a rush of adulation is a heady, scary, remarkably powerful experience, one she is not likely to forget all her life long. That crush can be on a teacher (*To Sir With Love*), on a rock god (*Bye Bye Birdie*), on a seemingly unattainable older man (*Sabrina*), or on the very idea of being in love and being loved back (*Smooth Talk*). Why, she can even have a crush on a horse (*National Velvet*), as every girl knows.

Ann-Margret, and her famous midriff, in *Bye Bye Birdie*, torn between the dangerous sexuality offered by an Elvis-like rock star (Jesse Pearson) and one boy, one special boy (Bobby Rydell).

Bye Bye Birdie
1963

Who is that running endlessly toward us on an invisible treadmill against a stark blue background? Why, it's Ann-Margret, simply *crushed* that her favorite rock star has been drafted into the Army! *"I'll miss the way you smile, as though it's just for me, and each and every night, I'll write you faithfully!"* she sings.

The phenomenon of mass teenage hero worship is lampooned in *Bye Bye Birdie*, a sharp musical comedy that knows the sexual yearnings of a young girl's midriff.

And before we address anything else, we have to address Ann-Margret's midriff. In 1963 there was nothing to equal it—at least not for young girls who wanted desperately to grow up to be Ann-Margret, to wear those Capri pants, to bust loose of the constraints of Sweetapple, Ohio, or wherever they currently lived. Scratch many women today and you'll find a little kitten with a whip.

Ann-Margret plays sweet Kim MacAfee from Sweetapple. She's a girl who makes sex look both dangerous and fun. She begins the movie as a tomboy who dates "one boy, one special boy, one boy to laugh with and joke with, have Coke with." Once the Elvis-like pop star Conrad Birdie (Jesse Pearson) is ensconced in her suburban home—drinking beer for breakfast, swiveling his hips as an aid to locomotion, and irritating Kim's excitable dad—Kim's hormones start revving up like the motorcycle Conrad rode in on.

Down comes the hair! Out comes the midriff! She's gotta lotta livin' to do!

Swedish showgirl Ann-Margaret Olsson was twenty-two when she made *Bye Bye Birdie*. She was young enough to play the typical teenager chosen at random to receive Conrad's last public kiss before his Army stint. The actress was also old enough to bring real sexual danger to the scene in which she threatens to *"drink champagne as though it were water!"*

The plan is to have Conrad sing struggling songwriter Dick Van Dyke's tune on *The Ed Sullivan Show*, then give Kim a kiss seen 'round the world. There are a hundred and one flies in the ointment, including Kim's media-hound dad (Paul Lynde), a molasses-slow Russian ballet, Kim's angry boyfriend (Bobby Rydell), the songwriter's angry girlfriend (Janet Leigh), and various jealousies and misunderstandings.

One part of the movie that could definitely be cut is the choreographed gang rape. Don't remember that scene? That's where Janet Leigh, trying to make her boyfriend jealous, all too successfully seduces the attendees of a Shriners' convention. As the music heats up, the Shriners gang up on her until they are all under the table together or tossing her from one to the other as she fights them off. The undertone of the piece is nasty and frightening.

Compare that with the light, brilliant "Honestly Sincere" number in which Conrad effortlessly makes every woman for miles faint dead away from his sex appeal. Conrad finishes his song to a town square of fallen females and failed hearts as far as the eye can see. This nod to the battlefield scene in *Gone With the Wind* is just one of many clever homages that director George Sidney inserted for the amusement of film buffs. Biographer Eric Monder reports that Sidney and producer Fred Kohlmar "created the largest mobile boom ever built" to shoot that scene (all of whose comic effect is lost in the pan-and-scan video version).

One vindication of the film's sexiness is that the spring 1964 issue of *Film Quarterly* called the movie "more startling and obscene than anything you will find in the ripest of art films."

Conrad Birdie turns out to be beside the point. Its heart, soul, and midriff belong to Ann-Margret as she makes that delicate transition from Daddy's little girl to sex kitten. Females of all ages can watch Ann-Margret change blithely from a frilly dress to a sloppy sweatshirt and reflect on how lovely to be a woman.

National Velvet

1944

There is no love so enduring as that between a girl and her horse, at least not for any girl who has been through puberty. *National Velvet* speaks to the equine obsessions of girls everywhere. It also spoke to the career obsessions of Elizabeth Taylor, who was only eleven years old when she first put herself forward for the role.

Taylor fought hoof and mane for the role of Velvet Brown, the girl who rides her horse to victory. She went after the part with the same single-mindedness with which Velvet goes after the Grand National. Although better-known actresses were up for the role, including Katharine Hepburn, Shirley Temple, and Margaret Sullavan, Taylor was undeterred.

Producer Pandro Berman thought Elizabeth didn't have enough of a body to be believable as the "bit of a girl clutching the neck of a bandy-legged outsider" who "streaked across the line to win the greatest race in turfdom." According to C. David Heymann's biography *Liz*, she confronted producer Berman and said, "Don't worry, you'll have your breasts."

In addition to riding lessons, she embarked on a concerted course of power eating and chest-enlargement exercises. Luckily, she was at an age where nature takes its course, and when she next showed up on the studio lot, she had put on an extra couple of inches in more than one direction.

Costar Mickey Rooney, who was twenty-three at the time, has disputed Taylor's claim about her dramatic fall from "the Pi"; he has said that like all the movie's daredevil scenes, it was orchestrated by stunt double Billy Cartlidge. (Australian jockey Snowy Baker doubled for the final race scene.)

National Velvet did what it was meant to do; it made Taylor a star at M-G-M after just a handful of movies. For a souvenir, she kept the horse

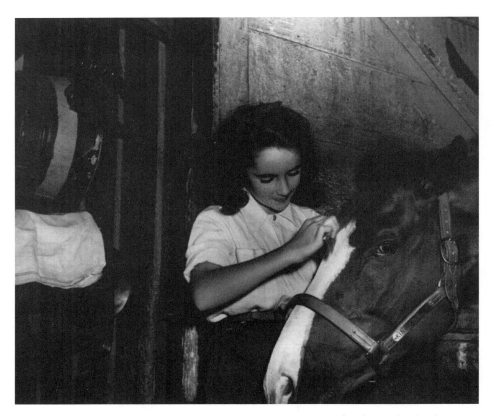

Nothing comes between a girl and her horse in *National Velvet*. Elizabeth Taylor spent a summer trying to develop a slight bustline in order to qualify for the role.

and years later joked to Berman during a chance meeting that she was "still paying for feed for that goddamned nag."

The Freudian interpretation of horse love, naturally, is from a male point of view—that it represents a girl's wish for a penis. But from a female point of view, it is about harnessing and controlling power with one's thighs, and men certainly don't corner the market on that. While men get off on their power to penetrate, women get off on their power to envelop.

National Velvet also doubles as a story of subversive matriarchal strength. Anne Revere won a Supporting Actress Oscar for playing Velvet's sensible mom, a former swimming champion herself, who gently but firmly enables Velvet to realize her dreams by blocking patriarch

Donald Crisp's narrow-minded edicts. Velvet's father is all for making the Pi (short for Pirate) into a cart horse or turning him into glue until Mrs. Brown intervenes.

"You have only your faces for your fortunes," he admonishes his daughters (including Angela Lansbury, the eldest).

Mom uses the money she saved all those years from her swimming medals to help pay Velvet's entry fee in the race, thus passing along her own championship dreams to her daughter.

At first, Velvet wants to race for the good of Pi, a noble horse that deserves the chance. Later, when she disguises herself as a male jockey in order to run the race herself, she stops displacing her real feelings. She covets "the glory of winning," as well she should.

"I wish your mother were here," says Rooney, her trainer, who also happens to be the son of the man who coached her mother to victory all those years before.

"She is here," says Velvet. "She's here inside me."

Velvet's unshakable faith in her horse is really her faith in herself. "He'll be an enchanted horse with invisible wings who will take me over every jump if I were to ride him," she proclaims.

She rides. She wins. She is disqualified, not just because she's a girl but because she falls off the horse before she reaches the enclosure. (She falls off because she has a penchant for fainting whenever her happiness is too great to contain.)

"Mother, we won!" Velvet announces on her return, bypassing all the other well-wishers. "Were we the best in the world, Mother?"

Mom, sensing that the word "we" does not refer to girl and horse but to mother and daughter, reassures her.

"Yes, the best in the world."

Sabrina

1954, 1995

Ten years before Audrey Hepburn endured a complete makeover in *My Fair Lady*, she was utterly transformed in *Sabrina*, thus, in both cases, winning the men who couldn't see her virtues before the change. Conspiracy theorists might blame the cosmetics industry.

Sabrina, a 1954 Billy Wilder romantic comedy, remade by Sydney Pollack in 1995, is a simple Cinderella story that is for women the cinematic equivalent of comfort food. A lowly chauffeur's daughter with a lifelong crush on the playboy who resides in the big house goes away to Paris heartsick, comes back a babe, and nabs the older brother instead.

Sabrina watches from the security of a tree limb in the garden as David, the younger of the Larrabee heirs, romances one girl after another, spiriting them off with champagne and a dance. In the original, Hepburn is so distraught over not being taken seriously by William Holden that she inhales the exhaust of all eight of the Larrabee family cars. The remake couldn't cope with Sabrina's cracked psyche and with such an old-fashioned idea of romantic anguish, so they simply make Julia Ormond shy, awkward, and miserable with yearning—nothing that hitting her twenties wouldn't cure.

Both versions pack her off to Paris, where Hepburn takes cooking classes, learning to crack eggs with one hand, and Ormond interns for *Vogue*, learning to lose the frump and get with the fashion. Either way, Sabrina returns to the Long Island Larrabee estate with just enough Paris polish to woo David away from his betrothed. (The original was filmed on the actual Glen Cove estate of Paramount president Barney Balaban.)

Now, when David puts two champagne flutes in his back pocket and steals off to the solarium, it's to meet Sabrina, who has returned from Paris with the best accent, evening wear, and manners of any of the local

118

Being nearly two generations apart doesn't faze Humprey Bogart or Audrey Hepburn, shown here on the set of the 1954 romantic love triangle *Sabrina*.

possibilities. David famously sits on the glasses by mistake, resulting in a prolonged glass-shards-in-tush routine. This puts a crimp in David's courting style — and, in the remake, in Greg Kinnear's career as a Gap T-shirt model. "Marriage?" Kinnear muses aloud in one of the many snappy one-liners designed for the 1990s audience. "I know what that is. That thing where you hang together a lot."

The Larrabee family dispatches Linus, David's elder, sober-sided brother, to deal with the Sabrina problem; David's impending marriage is important to an upcoming business merger, and the Larrabees are all about money. Linus is a repressed workaholic, "the world's only living heart donor," who is rusty at the fine art of love.

In both versions, Linus is shockingly older than the barely-out-of-her-teens Sabrina. Both Humphrey Bogart and Harrison Ford were in their mid-fifties when they essayed the part of Linus Larrabee —*calling Dr. Freud*! (Even Holden, as the playboy, was thirty-six at the time, nearly old enough to be Sabrina's father.)

Sabrina is an example of one of women's favorite revenge fantasies — that the guy who wouldn't give you a second look would someday come begging when you have blossomed into the belle of the ball. Marrying the guy's smarter older brother is a good idea, too — something that will really rub his nose in it for years to come.

The Sabrina who comes wafting home from Paris is as fine and cultured a woman as you'd ever want to meet. (Of all the original Oscar

The older man, 1996 style: Chauffeur's daughter Julia Ormond makes businessman Harrison Ford feel like a teenager again in the updated *Sabrina*.

nominations, only Edith Head won for costume design.) She is so perfect the movie feels like a fantasy. Both versions end with Sabrina taking off for happiness everlasting with Linus. But in the psychological realm, at least for women, the movie ends with the feeling that the gawking teenager is still up a tree, daydreaming possible flamboyant palliatives for the pain of her obsession.

Smooth Talk

1985

Adolescent girls are rarely understood by anyone, including themselves. Filled with inchoate sexual yearnings and alternately delighted and alarmed by their budding bodies, these girls face being treated like children at home and like sexually knowledgable adults by boys and men.

At this age, a girl's looks are deceiving. She sends signals she isn't aware of, she encourages men without appreciating the consequences, and her friends, maturing at different rates, drift away. One day you're sneaking off to the beach with your girlfriends; the next, you're crossing the highway to where the older kids do grown-up things, like "parking."

One of the best movies to represent the precariousness of this time in a girl's life is *Smooth Talk*, Joyce Chopra's tender adaptation of a Joyce Carol Oates short story. It shows a summer crossroads in the life of Connie (Laura Dern), a gangly, awkward fifteen-year-old who is just discovering the power of her body over men.

Every day, Connie and her friends lie to their parents about going to the mall and the movies; they are really using their time to dress tartily and scope out boys. They change clothes and apply makeup in the mall rest rooms, then careen around, giggling, flirting, and trying to puzzle out the ways of older girls.

An example of how Connie is misunderstood at home is that after her father catches her crossing the highway to the hot-dog drive-in where the older teens hang out, he gives her a talking to. She thinks he has guessed that she is spending her evenings necking with boys. Instead, since he still thinks of her as a child, he chides her for crossing the highway away from the intersection. "I look right in your eyes and all I see are a bunch of trashy daydreams," accuses her mother.

Meanwhile, Connie has settled into the crosshairs of a much older boy, Arnold Friend, the kind of soulless jerk young girls fall for before

Laura Dern is only beginning to see what effect her developing body is having on boys, much to her detriment, in *Smooth Talk*.

they understand the type. It is Arnold's dangerous "smooth talk" that lures Connie out of her parents' house one afternoon to lose her virginity.

Actually, it's a rape—in all but the legal sense. And the tense, uncomfortable scene leading up to it is nauseating to a female audience. There is also an excitement in seeing such a seduction filmed for what it really is—a violation of a girl by using her own unsteadiness against her.

Connie never locks the screen door that stands between her and Arnold. She is frightened and also intrigued by being singled out as special and by Arnold's promise that he knows her true heart and can give her what she needs.

Men often misread this scene, just the way they misinterpret the physical cues that fly off young girls' bodies. One male reviewer summed up the movie as being about Connie's attempts to lose her virginity. He must have missed the part where she tries to tell her estranged older sister why she goes after boys: "The boys are so nice to you. Did you ever have a boy hold you close and sing to you?"

To Sir With Love
1967

"Do you shake?" asks precocious high schooler Pamela Dare (Judy Geeson) the first time she meets Mark Thackeray, her new teacher. In sixties' parlance, she is asking him whether he wants to dance.

To Sir With Love was released in 1967, and the language, clothing, and attitudes are now embarrassingly dated. No matter. The movie, like "those schoolgirl days" promised by the title song, "will still live on and on."

Columbia Pictures never understood why *To Sir With Love* became such a hit. Research teams handed out audience questionnaires and concluded it must be due to handsome Sidney Poitier—*hello*!

Another reason girls swooned was that they had stood in Pamela Dare's shoes, adoring from afar the one teacher who singled them out, cared about them, made them feel womanly. In every girl's life there is a teacher who has taken her from crayons to perfume.

And that song! Lulu, who was "introduced" in this movie, stayed on the charts and in girlish hearts, with those adolescent yearnings tinged with gratitude and lust. *"If you wanted the moon, I would write across the sky in letters that would soar a thousand feet high: To sir, with love..."*

Judy Geeson, with her half-moon eyes and bee-stung lips, plays "Miss Dare," the lovestruck high school senior in London's rough East End. The new teacher, a would-be engineer who can't get a job because of the color of his skin, defers to the rowdy students by their last names in order to give them a sense of self-respect. They in turn call him Sir.

In just weeks he makes them productive members of society while learning that he is more needed as a teacher than an engineer.

Movies about inner-school kids, from *The Blackboard Jungle* to *Dangerous Minds*, lose their edge quicker than teenagers lose their virginity. The rough kids of *To Sir With Love* seem hilariously well behaved and cooperative from today's perspective. This is not as bothersome as you'd

Sidney Poitier transfixes his tough inner-city students even when he is simply teaching them how to make a salad in *To Sir With Love*.

think, since what truly fuels the movie is not Sir's career arc but the child-woman Pamela's desperately sweet crush.

"I am sick of your foul language, your crude behavior, and your sluttish manner!" explodes the normally reserved teacher when he finds the girls burning a sanitary napkin. From then on, he's a caring disciplinarian, just what the fatherless Miss Dare needs. "No man likes a slut for long. Only the worst type will marry one!"

Soon Pamela is bustling about Sir's desk, trying to tidy it up, gingerly offering herself to him. (He refuses, gentleman that he is.) "Don't make any mistake about Pamela," warns a fellow teacher. "She's a woman in every sense of the word!"

Despite such prim moral observations, the movie provides the ultimate frisson at the graduation dance. Pamela, having exacted a promise from Sir to call her by her first name, walks straight through a crowd of her peers to collect her dance with him. He "shakes," after all.

In the background, the Mindbenders are singing, appropriately enough, "It's Getting Harder All the Time."

CATFIGHTS

Men enjoy seeing the kind of physical "catfight" in which there's hair pulling; they either find it hilarious or a turn-on. Women, on the other hand, enjoy watching rivalries among women because it is such an emotionally charged, anxiety-producing arena. Screen catfights can achieve the kind of resolution so difficult in real life. The victor often wins the battle but loses the war, as in *All About Eve* and *Raise the Red Lantern*. Elizabeth Taylor never had a chance in *Ivanhoe*. Other women's men are the ultimate prize in *The Women* and *Working Girl*.

The classic catfight: Theater's *grandes dames* Bette Davis (*left*) and Anne Baxter go at it with claws barely retracted in *All About Eve*.

All About Eve
1950

The younger rival who insinuates herself into your life and supplants you is every woman's nightmare. This is the demon who co-opts your friends, seduces your man, trades on your style, and studies you for tips on how to get what you have. You invite her in. Once comfortable in your life, she sucks your soul. In psychology they might call her an "as if" personality, a sponge without the inner resources to cultivate a personality of her own. In movies, they call her Eve Harrington.

Bette Davis called her the "sweet bitch." Eve Harrington (Anne Baxter) hangs around the stagedoor after every performance by theater star Margo Channing (Davis) until Margo's friend (Celeste Holm) brings her in for an introduction. Eve, already an actress in the making, reduces everyone to tears with her hard-luck story. Out of pity (the flattery doesn't hurt, either), Margo takes in Eve as a personal assistant.

Eve proves eerily efficient. She not only takes Margo's dresses to the cleaners; she holds them up in the mirror to see how they'd look on her. She not only remembers Margo's boyfriend's birthday and places a phone call to him on behalf of the self-centered Margo; she also sends a private telegram of her own.

Not everyone is fooled. The no-nonsense maid, played by Thelma Ritter, can see right through Eve. "She thinks only of me, doesn't she?" asks Davis, just beginning to test her doubts.

"Well, let's say she thinks *about* you, anyway, like she's studying ya! Like you was a play or a book or a set of blueprints, how you walk, talk, act, what you eat!"

The boyfriend thinks of Eve as a "stagestruck kid." The best friend thinks Eve is so harmless, she actually engineers a kind of palace coup. She makes Davis so late for a performance that Eve, her understudy in all senses of the word, slips into her shoes and parlays that into a career that has her at the beginning and end of the movie accepting a prestigious theater award that should have gone by rights to her mentor.

By then, everyone has caught on to Eve's true nature. Now they must all live with the monster they created. Everyone is held to the lie by gentle coercion or by actual blackmail.

"Funny business, a woman's career," says Davis on realizing that Eve is after her boyfriend. "Sooner or later, we've got to work at it no matter how many other careers we've had or wanted."

The script is filled with wonderfully bitchy innuendo. "She apologized, didn't she?" a playwright implores his wife about Eve's secret visit to him. "On her knees, no doubt" is the reply.

In real life, all sorts of Eveish shenanigans were going on. Davis won the part after Claudette Colbert broke her back and, though she denied it, played it much like her own theater rival Tallulah Bankhead. Davis and Gary Merrill, who played her boyfriend, became offscreen lovers and banded together against everyone else on the set. (They later married.) Davis and Celeste Holm despised each other; Holm plays Davis's best friend, who betrays her when she arranges Eve's debut in Margo's place.

The accepted critical thinking is that director Joe Mankiewicz used *All About Eve* to get out his jollies on the subject of the theater, a topic near and dear to him. Theater life, in all its onstage glory and backstage strife, preoccupied him. Dialogue disparaging the actors, who are but the instruments of the underappreciated writers, abounds.

But if anything, Joe was the Eve in his older brother Herman's life. Herman, coauthor of *Citizen Kane*, was considered the famous one in the family. Joe worked like the dickens to outshine him and succeeded. Herman may have been the more talented one, but Joe gets the glory today. Struggles to ascend to the throne and keep it make for timeless stories that are not unique to females.

Yet *All About Eve* hits a nerve. When one woman tries to supplant another, it is usually in ways only women themselves can recognize—the appropriation of a certain style, of clothes and mannerisms, all cloaked in a calculated innocence and sweetness that men find erotic and that other women find manipulative. In *All About Eve* the women catch on first, the men last, but everyone eventually finds out that Eve is a snake. In real life, things aren't so neat.

Ivanhoe

1952

As mentioned elsewhere in this book (see *Witness*), tending a man's wounds is one of the greatest examples of foreplay the cinema can offer women. As Robert Taylor lies unconscious beneath the ministering hands of Elizabeth Taylor in *Ivanhoe*, his eyelids flutter, and Liz speaks aloud her thoughts. "I love you! And I must not feel it! And yet I love you, Ivanhoe, with all the longing in the lonely world!"

She must see to it that she not feel this love, for she is Rebecca, the lowly Jewess, and Robert Taylor is Ivanhoe, the Saxon knight whose mission is to restore the Norman king Richard the Lionhearted to his rightful throne. "The knight's faith forbids him to look on you as a woman," her father warns her, further fanning the flames of desire. Oh, Ivanhoe, Ivanhoe, wherefore art thou Ivanhoe?

Ivanhoe already has a flaxen-haired Saxon maiden waiting in the wings. "Does a Jew feel jealousy?" wonders the simpering Rowena (Joan Fontaine), who doesn't get out much. "Then she is not so different from a Saxon, after all." Ah, the sweet stirrings of twelfth-century political correctness.

When Ivanhoe is wounded in a joust, Rebecca bars Rowena's way at the first-aid tent. "Stand aside, for *you?*" says Rowena huffily. "No, milady," answers Rebecca. "For Ivanhoe."

Make that *Sir* Ivanhoe, the original knight in shining armor. No wonder the girls are both hoping to make a dent in his armor.

Rebecca is a cloistered girl who breathes the air of love and adventure when this white knight comes galloping into her life. Rebecca gets all of Ivanhoe's attentions for most of the movie until she nobly accepts her lowly social and religious status and hands him back over to Rowena. Before she relinquishes him, she makes plenty of romantic inroads.

Those lips! Those eyes! But they're not enough in the twelfth century for Robert Taylor to choose Elizabeth Taylor, despite her prayers, in the romantic joust *Ivanhoe*.

Because of her renowned beauty—and with the young Elizabeth Taylor, they ain't kidding—Rebecca has led a sheltered life, unapt to toil and trouble in the world. Along comes Ivanhoe, seeking the kidnaped King Richard. He rescues Rebecca's elderly dad, and in return, the father promises to raise the money Ivanhoe needs to free Richard. Rebecca is hiding all the while behind the curtains, because "the brightest lights are kept hidden," but you can just imagine her thinking like one of those old Warner Bros. cartoons: "A *MAN!*" With the word "man" taking up two syllables.

And what a man, what a man, what a mighty fine man. Handsome, chivalrous, he can as easily sit a horse as unseat an opponent. He'll fight for your honor—and here's the exciting part—to the death!

Rebecca shows up at Ivanhoe's lodgings alone one night to hand him, uh, the family jewels. She is donating her dead mother's inheritance to Ivanhoe's royal cause.

Now we pause for much battling and jousting, all the stuff the male audience likes. There's that subplot involving King Richard to contend with. Then we can return to the important stuff: Ivanhoe fighting to the death for the honor of the raven-haired, violet-eyed Rebecca.

Interestingly, neither of the Taylors, Elizabeth nor Robert, wanted to make this on-location M-G-M spectacle. Elizabeth didn't like second billing, and Robert preferred westerns. Still, the movie did well at the box office, luring men for the jousts and women for the love triangle.

While Ivanhoe is off fighting, both Rebecca and Rowena are menaced by dastardly suitors who threaten their virginity. Almost like a French farce, Ivanhoe must rescue both women from such nasty fates.

The time is drawing nigh for Ivanhoe to go back to Rowena the fair (and largely uninteresting), so the movie throws us another bone. Rebecca's new suitor (George Sanders) wants her so badly that he, too, would die for her. You have to admire that, even in a spineless villain.

We swerve now from the adrenaline rush of men who would lay down their lives for you to that hobgoblin of romantic longing—unrequited love. "You must blame the fates that it was I who loved you and not Ivanhoe," the new suitor gasps to Rebecca before dying.

Now she sees the error of her ways. Ivanhoe, for whom her eyes shine, always planned to return to the more suitable Rowena (the way men usually return to their wives, even though they claim it gives them no pleasure). In her blind faith in Ivanhoe, Rebecca has now lost her own opportunity for happiness.

The men may fight to the death, but the female rivals do the equivalent of the obligatory handshake after a tennis match. They embrace. "His heart was always yours," says Rebecca, conceding. You have to admire (from afar, at least) the woman who takes the high road.

Raise the Red Lantern

1992

In the ancient Greek play *Lysistrata*, women realize they have strength in numbers. They deny their men sex in order to get the social changes they desire.

Fast-forward to the twentieth century and you have women fighting tooth and nail over men they ordinarily wouldn't look at twice just because a man on the arm (or its corollary, a ring on the finger) is still considered a woman's ultimate status symbol.

Since women do not align themselves in a vertical hierarchy—as men do in sports and the military—the fight for men often appears to be a free-for-all among equals. It takes a movie from China to show what this particular catfight is really about. In the Oscar-nominated *Raise the Red Lantern*, the powerless will do nearly anything for a tiny piece of the pie, even if it means contributing to their own weakness.

Asian screen goddess Gong Li stars as a reluctant teenage concubine of a middle-aged man who already has three wives. The women fight each other, their only possible allies, over this man they hardly know.

The movie opens in extreme close-up as Songlian (Gong Li), a nineteen-year-old university student of the 1920s who doesn't have the money to finish her studies, stoically tells her stepmother that she's leaving to become a concubine. "Isn't that a woman's fate?" she asks rhetorically as tears creep down her face.

As the newest wife—known to the other wives as Fourth Sister—Songlian is immediately iced out. She represents even more competition for the dubious honor of getting the master to spend the night.

The title of the movie comes from the practice of hanging huge, jolly red lanterns in the courtyard outside the apartment of the chosen mistress of the night, the wife on whom the master will bestow his favors. Those favors alone may not be so special—we never even see the master's face clearly in the movie—but the chosen woman gets a few minor trappings of her temporary victory. She gets a foot massage, performed with tiny cymbal-hammers, whose shimmering insect sound fills the air and drives the neglected wives nuts with envy.

Moreover, the chosen one gets to decide the next day's menu, of no small importance when one of them happens to be a vegetarian.

Power is a relative thing. The servant girl wants only to be a concubine. The concubine wants only to be the favorite concubine. The favorite concubine wants only to be the mother of a son. In this insulated, stratified society, the four wives compete with dead earnestness to be top dog, one night at a time.

Each wife has a bag of tricks to keep the master happy. One of them gives a mean massage and secretly hatches plots. Another feigns illness in the middle of the night to divert the master's attention; she also keeps a secret lover. As soon as Songlian catches on to the backstage machinations of her rivals, she pretends she is pregnant. With the possibility of a son and heir on the way, the master chooses Songlian time and again.

China's national treasure, actress Gong Li, collapses when she realizes the part she has played in betraying sisterhood in *Raise the Red Lantern*. (Courtesy of Photofest)

Her lanterns are lit night and day, and the shimmering insect sound floats from her window into the courtyard that is shared by all the wives.

Songlian is betrayed by her own menstrual blood. More precisely, she is betrayed by the serving girl who sees the blood and turns her in. In their rivalry for a man they scarcely know and certainly couldn't care much about, the women turn on each other, with mortal consequences for two of them.

Director Zhang Yimou is the most commercial, internationally successful Chinese director and also the most controversial. While we in the West are free to interpret his movies as parables about gender injustice, the Chinese government has banned, censored, or restricted his movies because of their political overtones.

The theme of women being unwitting accomplices in their own subjugation recurs in the director's work. Perhaps that is the best (and safest) metaphor Zhang could find for the oppression of the masses.

The Women
1939

The opening credits of *The Women* introduce the players by their corresponding zoo animals — Norma Shearer the sweet lamb, Rosalind Russell the feline, etc. Although the movie sums up with Joan Crawford calling the ladies a word that "is seldom used in high society, outside of a kennel," the characters have nothing canine about them. They're all catty.

Director George Cukor's catfight nonpareil exaggerates the stereotype of women as duplicitous backstabbers. Although it's certainly a depiction that females resent, *The Women* is so playful, spirited, and funny that women are naturally drawn to it.

It also, not coincidentally, is one of the few movies not to contain a single man in the cast. Even the men these women are squabbling over are never seen.

The movie, based on the Clare Boothe play, sides with Norma Shearer, a devoted wife and mother — a "woman" as opposed to a "female." She's the last person in town to know that her husband is cheating on her with conniving perfume countergirl Joan Crawford. Shearer's "friends," a group of fabulous gossips whose chatter reaches such levels as to create a sort of indecipherable white-noise effect, see to it that Shearer finds out. Then they track every humiliation and confrontation that Shearer endures on her way to a Reno divorce.

Meanwhile, all the women are exchanging husbands in an escalating game of musical chairs. The divorce farm in Reno, run by Marjorie Main, is a revolving door of rich, vacuous society ladies from New York. Rosalind Russell is there at the same time as Paulette Goddard, the one who is stealing her husband. The women change men as often as they change their couturier plumage.

In fact, it is in a dressing room that Shearer finally confronts the Other Woman; each is charging her wardrobe to the account of the same

Rosalind Russell gets a coat of Jungle Red nail polish plus all the latest dirt on her close, dear friends in *The Women*.

man. "When anything I wear doesn't please Mr. Haines," Crawford taunts Mr. Haines's current wife, "I take it off."

The Women is as much about men's urges to cheat as it is about women's urges to help them do it. "A man has only one escape from his old self," advises Shearer's wise-owl mom (Lucile Watson). "To see a different self in the mirror of some woman's eyes."

"The first man to figure out how he can love his wife *and* another woman is gonna win that prize they're always giving out in Sweden," philosophizes another character.

Director Cukor, known for his ability to work with actresses, brought out sparkling performances from his cast, particularly Rosalind Russell, who steals scenes right and left.

The movie's apparent moral, voiced by Shearer as she rushes back into the arms of her errant husband, is that a woman must put aside her own pride in order to cling to the comfort of a marriage. Pride is "a luxury a woman in love can't afford," she says.

This unpleasant message isn't as self-effacing as it seems. Shearer only regains her husband after resorting to the same awful tricks of her litter of friends. She paints her nails the same "Jungle Red" and uses gossip, innuendo, spying, and manipulation to unmask Crawford as the gold digger that she is. So the little lamb was just a cat in sheep's clothing, after all.

It doesn't say much for the power of men to recognize true love or to appreciate a woman's inner qualities. But while it paints females in a negative light, it also points out the pressures on working-class women to fight for the social stature that an alliance with the right man can give them. The women of *The Women* know that it's a jungle out there, and they'll need sharp Jungle Red claws to survive.

Working Girl

1988

What does Tess McGill really want as she daydreams her way to work each morning on the Staten Island Ferry?

One could argue that she wants to move out of the secretarial pool and into a Wall Street trainee program; that's what the movie says so plainly. Isn't *Working Girl* about one plucky kid moving up the class, social, and career ladders with the agility of a Flying Wallenda?

Actually, *Working Girl* is a simple wish fulfillment fantasy that works closer to the bone than that. What Tess wants is what all girls secretly once wanted but were too afraid to go for: She wants to get rid of Mommy so she can have Daddy all to herself.

If you insist on reading the movie literally, then it is a comedy about a determined working girl (Melanie Griffith) who figures out how to get her foot in the door of corporate America. Lose the big hair, the borough accent, the tricolor eye shadow. Soften what needs to be softened (voice, body); harden what needs to be hardened (conscience, grit). Then reel in the mergers and acquisitions of the soulless 1980s.

All that still doesn't explain why women love this movie, why they can see it as many times as Carly Simon's inspirational (and Oscar-winning) "Let the River Run" plays on the soundtrack. And it certainly doesn't explain why those women who cheer Tess's final defeat of her "bony-assed" female boss (Sigourney Weaver) feel an odd sensation of having crossed the line and betrayed themselves.

In the Electra complex that is *Working Girl*, Tess is the little girl who can't grow up. Her hair, clothes, and makeup all suggest a child playing dress-up. No one takes her seriously—not at work, where every seeming opportunity turns out to be another pimping assignment, and not at home, where boyfriend Alec Baldwin gives her sexy lingerie meant for his own satisfaction. "Can't you ever give me something I could wear outside?"

Melanie Griffith looks up to boss (and mommy figure) Sigourney Weaver in
Working Girl; **that is, until she steals Weaver's man, job, and status.**

Tess complains in her little-girl voice. (This is one film where Griffith's
underage voice is perfectly matched to the role.)

Tess finally becomes secretary to someone she'd very much like to
grow up to be—Katharine Parker (Weaver), a more sophisticated version
of Tess. Katharine is the adult of the two. She is elegant, glamorous, successful, and well-spoken. The movie (and Weaver's self-mocking performance) make it plain that all these qualities are wasted on a woman like
Katharine, who is insincere—a deadly sin in a movie in which fates will
be judged by one's ability to maintain a childlike honesty.

When Tess stays at Katharine's fancy town house, playing dress-up
in Mommy's clothes and imitating Mommy's ways, she discovers that
Katharine was going to go ahead with one of Tess's acquisition ideas and
then claim it as her own.

This gives Tess license to turn against Katharine and play grown-up
in the real world. She wears Katharine's six-thousand-dollar new dress,
attends a networking party under Katharine's name, and manages to pick
up none other than Katharine's own boyfriend. And if Katharine is the

mommy Tess wants so desperately to displace, you know what that makes Harrison Ford's character in the family constellation.

"I've got a head for business and a bod for sin," Tess tells Jack at the bar, where he is entranced by her honesty and the fact that she hasn't dressed in an intimidating, mannish way.

As Jack Trainer, Ford plays a man who has been belittled and emasculated by Katharine. "Can little Jack come out to play?" Katharine wheedles him, trying to reach inside his zipper. Jack needs a woman like Tess, someone he can trust, someone who will wipe the hot-dog mustard off his chin on the street.

Tess doesn't simply get a promotion, the ostensible goal of the movie. She strips her former boss of everything, from her man to her corner office. Everyone gleefully joins in booting Katharine out by her "bony ass." Tess is movin' on up, and women can relax to the fantasy, knowing that Tess got what she really wanted, after all.

And a better job, too!

DADDY DEAREST

A girl's first love is her father, and she searches for him among men the rest of her life, sometimes with success, sometimes to her detriment. The little princesses of *A Little Princess*, *The Professional*, *To Kill a Mockingbird*, and *A Tree Grows in Brooklyn* show what it's like to be Daddy's little girl, even when Daddy is a surrogate or leaves the scene prematurely. *Jane Eyre* shows what logically happens when a girl grows up searching in vain for a father figure.

Joan Fontaine's Jane—pining for affection from someone, anyone—is particularly vulnerable to Orson Welles's romantically distant Rochester in the 1944 version of *Jane Eyre*.

Jane Eyre

1944, etc.

Jane Eyre is the stuff of gothic romance, a genre with a special fascination
for women both in novels and movies. In a gothic romance, a girl gener-
ally goes straight from the house of her father to the house of her (much
older) husband—out of the frying pan and into the fire, so to speak. The
frightening changeover from one man's care to another's is characterized
in gothic parlance by the brooding, unfathomable nature of the new man
and the scary, imposing nature of the mansion he lives in. All is resolved
when the man's secrets are explained and his distance turns out to harbor
love, after all. (The mansion's secrets are explained, too, but many gothic
romances sacrifice the house for the heroine's greater comfort.)

Jane is Charlotte Brontë's creation, and her story has been filmed
many times. The plain but headstrong English governess who falls in love
with her mysterious, forbidding employer has been played over the years
by Ethel Grand, Louise Vale, Mabel Ballin, Virginia Bruce, Joan Elan,
Susannah York—and, in 1996, by Charlotte Gainsbourg. But the 1944
version is the most famous, with sweet Peggy Ann Garner playing the
mistreated young orphan who grows up to be Joan Fontaine and to win
the love of Orson Welles.

"I'd let my arm be broken if it would make anyone love me!" proclaims the yearning young Jane to her only friend (an early role for Elizabeth Taylor, who dies posthaste of a tubercular cough).

Jane studies hard and grows up determined to leave the confines of
the cold-comfort farm she has lived in since childhood. She advertises
for a position as governess and gets only one response. It's from Edward
Rochester, a strange and brooding loner with a dark secret hidden in his
tower on the Yorkshire moors. "You have no talents," Jane's sadistic
headmaster says scornfully, trying to bully her into staying on at low pay

at the charity school. "Your disposition is dark and rebellious, your appearance insignificant!"

To achieve this insignificance, Fontaine wore her hair oddly, in a less puffy approximation of Princess Leia's earmuffs. But then, the ruggedly handsome Welles was supposed to be so ugly as Edward Rochester that when he asks Jane if she considers him handsome, she blurts out, "No!" before she remembers who is paying her that thirty pounds per annum.

Jane cares for little Margaret O'Brien, playing Rochester's princesslike French ward. The governess falls in love from afar with her erratic employer, just as Julie Andrews would with Christopher Plummer in *The Sound of Music* twenty-one years later—what we call today the Robin Williams syndrome, in which the nanny gets promoted to wife.

The secret in Thornfield Hall tower, of course, is that Rochester already has a wife. In a literary twist on the old "my wife doesn't understand me" routine, Rochester's first wife is totally mad, a cackling lunatic cum arsonist. (One could even say that the 1943 horror film *I Walked With a Zombie* is the Jane Eyre story all over again, set on a voodoo-laden Caribbean island where the zombified wife's nurse falls in love with the husband.)

In 1993 a bit of soft-core porn called *Wide Sargasso Sea* made an interesting case on behalf of the wife, imagining a woman whose sexuality is too threatening to her husband and who winds up a victim and prisoner in that turret, not a madwoman, after all, just an inconvenient wife to a man who loves another.

Nevertheless, the 1944 version keeps women on the side of the governess—virtuous, loving, not caring about Rochester's wealth or looks. "That, gentlemen, is my wife!" says Rochester with a flourish, showing off the lunatic in the turret when trying to justify why he was about to commit bigamy with the nanny. Everyone leaves the room in indignation, but there's no one who doesn't side with Rochester, or at least with Jane.

The mad wife, whom we never actually see (she is more awful in our imaginations), conveniently burns down the house and herself with it, leaving Jane free to pursue the now-blind Rochester. (In the 1996 Franco Zeffirelli remake, Maria Schneider plays the madwoman, a confirmed pyromaniac with a manic laugh.)

The romance of this scenario appeals to women on several levels, including the usual lure of the gothic. "Will you help me in my transformation from India rubber back to flesh?" asks Rochester early in the movie. Yes, yes! With just a little tinkering, Rochester could be the perfect man, and here he is willing to let Jane orchestrate the transformation!

There is also the idea of payback. Women who, like Jane, have been forced into caretaker roles when they should have been enjoying life hate to think that their time was wasted. A life of service and deprivation merits not only the man of one's dreams but one who is totally grateful and dependent—maybe because he is blind and ugly? Nothing less would satisfy.

Wide Sargasso Sea attempted to explain the "back story" of *Jane Eyre* by showing a young Rochester (Nathaniel Parker) romancing impressionable island girl Karina Lombard.

A Little Princess
1995

"Didn't anyone ever tell you that you're a princess?" asks Sara Crewe of her evil boarding-school mistress, who has locked her in a garret and taken away all her precious belongings. It is a bittersweet moment in *A Little Princess* because it truly reminds us that all women, no matter how aged and embittered, were once their daddy's little girls.

Shirley Temple rode this Frances Hodgson Burnett novel to movie victory in 1939, with Ian Hunter as the beloved daddy who is thought to have died in the war, leaving little Sara an orphan in a cruel world.

In 1995 the sweetly grave Liesel Matthews essayed the role in this beautifully mounted children's story that makes every female in the audience feel like a princess again.

Sara is the crown jewel of Captain Crewe's life. He pampers her, indulges her, encourages her imagination. They live in India, where Sara spins grandly passionate fairy tales for her friends.

When World War I is declared, the captain (Liam Cunningham) tenderly drops Sara off at the same New York boarding school where her late mother had been educated. Sara hates to see him go off to war, but she loves him so much that she has memorized his face; he is always a part of her.

Miss Minchin's School for Girls offers an elaborately rigid environment in which Sara is catered to because of her father's wealth but where imagination and girlish chatter are forbidden by the severe headmistress (Eleanor Bron). Nevertheless, Sara's spirit is indomitable. Soon she is entertaining her entranced, homesick schoolmates with stories and fancies that brighten their lives and give many of them—particularly the outcast black serving girl—hope for a better tomorrow.

When it is presumed that the captain has been killed in the war, Sara falls from the heights. She is moved mid-birthday party from her luxuri-

**Liesel Matthews's belief in daddy Liam Cunningham's
love enables her to survive reports of his death in
A Little Princess.**

ous bedroom to the attic with the other serving girl, divested of her trea-
sures and any reminders of Daddy, and made to polish the endless hard-
wood floors of the boarding school. The other girls are forbidden to
consort with her.

Her father had told her that every little girl is a princess, that it is her
birthright. For a while, Sara's faith in this hits a slump. But thanks to the
bolstering of her friends and all kinds of semimystical coincidences,
Daddy winds up recovering from his wounds in the house next door,
hampered only by an amnesia that has made him forget that he has a
daughter to rescue.

Shirley Temple rode the same material to movie victory in 1939's *The Little Princess*, with Ian Hunter as the beloved daddy who leaves her in a cruel orphanage.

If there's anything stronger than daddy love, it's fear of abandonment, and *A Little Princess* presses all the right buttons. Even a father who grunts distractedly from behind his morning newspaper couldn't be any more threatening to a little girl's sense of self than if he were a war hero stricken with amnesia. At least amnesia can be broken through by the force of a child's love. With other daddies, it is not so easy to have your face reflected in his.

Sara Crewe is a fabulous role model for the younger set. She is able to stand up to the resident bully (Sara pretends to put a curse on her so that her hair will fall out), humble enough not to drive away friends who would normally choke with envy, sharp enough to outwit the headmistress, patient enough to withstand injustice, and loyal enough to reward the little people. (Even the youthful chimney sweep is a beneficiary of Sara's foresight.)

If a little girl is all these things and more, will her father never, ever, leave her? *A Little Princess* takes this horrible childhood fear to the brink and safely back.

The Professional
1994

Humbert had his Lolita. Maurice Chevalier had his Gigi. Now Leon has his Mathilde.

Who knows the dark secrets of the love that binds little girls to father figures? In *The Professional*, Leon, a cold-blooded French hit man who sleeps sitting up in a chair, has an admirer in the neighbor-girl Mathilde. In its own twisted way, what Leon does for the love of this child rivals Humphrey Bogart giving up Ingrid Bergman on the tarmac of *Casablanca*.

As the movie opens, the camera rises over Central Park like a panther springing from the urban jungle, with the swiftness and certainty of a highly skilled professional. A professional "cleaner," that is—someone like the meticulous hit man Leon. When you need someone rubbed out with no fuss, no muss, you go to Leon.

"Are you free Tuesday?" asks a man who desires a hit.

"I'm free Tuesday," replies Leon. He's cool, impassive, very French.

This killing machine is the almost saintly hero of Luc Besson's edgy, strangely romantic thriller.

Besson is the French director who made the hormonal killer-babe movie *La Femme Nikita* in which Anne Parillaud is a wild child redeemed through a crash course in government-sanctioned assassination. *The Professional* is Besson's first American movie, and it combines the thrills of the Hollywood shoot-out with the morose introspection of a European art film.

Leon (the hangdog-faced Jean Reno) is a man totally devoted to his work. He owns nothing but a plant potted heavily in metaphor. His briefcase contains a miniarsenal. After a long day reforming underworld welchers, he treats himself to a glass of wholesome milk.

Tense, alert, humorless, he lives by a code of honor: no women, no children. That is, he neither kills women and children, nor does he enter-

Orphan Natalie Portman and scrupulous hit man Jean Reno create their own fractured family in *The Professional*.

tain them. He wouldn't know how; unlike a James Bond, Leon is only a professional within the narrow parameters of his job.

Into the locked sanctuary of his apartment and his heart walks Mathilde (Natalie Portman), a precocious twelve-year-old neighbor with a crush on him. Mathilde's dad happens to be a drug dealer. And when he and Mathilde's family are rubbed out by a bad cop, she shows incredible presence of mind by walking straight past her own door and knocking on Leon's, thus fooling the killers and inheriting a better daddy in the bargain.

Now Leon is saddled with an adolescent femme Nikita in the making. What follows is a delicate and uniquely sentimental perversion of the familiar scenario in which two damaged people heal each other.

The child tenderly cleans his guns and buys his milk. The killer patiently teaches her the art of rooftop sniping, leading to one of the movie's many blackly comic sequences when the child picks out for target practice a Clintonesque president who happens to be jogging around the Central Park reservoir.

Kinetically filmed in wide screen, *The Professional* is a tale of spiritual salvation as told in the amoral pop cadences of a rat-tat-tat action movie. The adolescent orphan redeems Leon by apprenticing herself to him, and he redeems her by giving her the fatherly love she never had.

The child is always trying to claim Leon's affection. Only near the end do we see how deeply she has touched him. The onetime emotionless killing machine sacrifices himself for Mathilde's safety, making himself forever a better daddy than the biological one who risked his whole family for his selfish criminal needs.

To Kill a Mockingbird
1962

To Kill a Mockingbird has had a profound effect on several generations. Adapted from the Harper Lee novel about a southern lawyer who defends a black man despite community pressure, the movie won Gregory Peck an Oscar for playing the principled, loving daddy that every little tomboy wants for her own.

Demi Moore named her firstborn Scout after the tough young protagonist of the story, which is more of a tribute to the movie than if she had adapted it for modern audiences the way she did *The Scarlet Letter*. If Moore had taken the same creative liberties with *Mockingbird*, Scout might have given pasty next-door neighbor Boo Radley a makeover and then grown up to marry him.

Mockingbird is too sacred a film text to play with like that. Mary Badham, sister of future director John Badham, was nine years old when she played the six-year-old Jean Louise "Scout" Finch, a tomboy whose insatiable curiosity about her world—1930s Alabama—leads her to discover (with Papa's help) all that's right, wrong, and shaded with gray.

In addition to all the things *To Kill a Mockingbird* is about—racism, injustice, small-town ignorance, and childhood itself—it is also about gaining new respect for Daddy.

"He's too old for anything!" Scout's older brother Jem (Philip Alford) complains about their widowed father, the upstanding but no-fun Atticus Finch (Gregory Peck). "He can do plenty of things!" a neighbor argues back.

Jem is more easily won over than Scout. When he sees Atticus throw his spectacles to the ground and kill a rabid dog with a single blast from a shotgun, Jem is hooked on his dad and begins to take on junior aspects of him. For instance, Jem refuses to obey Atticus when he feels it is his moral duty to stand by him in front of a lynch mob at the courthouse, thus putting principles before obedience.

Mary Badham spends the kind of quality time every little girl dreams of with daddy Gregory Peck, in *To Kill a Mockingbird*.

Scout, though only six, is a more complicated individual. A scrapper who'll take on anyone who calls her father a "nigger lover," it takes her longer to comprehend the vagaries of racism. Her blunt way of seeing things is disarming enough to break up a lynch mob when she focuses on one individual: "Hey, Mr. Cunningham, I said hey! Don't you remember me?" Yet she finds that things are not so black and white in the adult universe.

When Atticus takes the case of a black man accused of raping a white woman, the townsfolk, who have always admired him for his principles, turn on him out of fear and ignorance. Atticus proves in court that the black man is innocent and that poor, abused Mayella Ewell is covering for the beating her own father gave her. The jury of the black man's "peers" finds him guilty, anyway, and as Atticus leaves the courthouse, Scout is amazed to see that all the black people surrounding her in the upper gallery rise. "Miss Jean Louise, stand up," she is told. "Your father's passing." My father, the hero.

All summer long, the kids play and test limits. (Their friend, Dill, is a character based on the young Truman Capote, who was a pal of author

Harper Lee.) Most of the limits have to do with going near the spooky house of Boo Radley, a neighbor who has never been seen and who is said to be crazy and kept locked in the basement by his mean old father. Notice how the other people in town—Boo, Mayella—all have such dastardly dads. Although the Finches are nearly as poor as anybody, Scout is rich in male parenting.

By the end of the movie, Scout has internalized the lessons her daddy has been patiently teaching her, so much so that she gets to teach Atticus a little something, too. Atticus is ready to defend Boo Radley, the supposedly nutty neighbor, for killing the man who attacked Scout and broke Jem's arm. But Scout convinces him that putting a basically harmless creature like Boo on a witness stand would be a sin, like shooting a mockingbird for sport.

Scout sits on the porch swing with Boo, her secret friend, and for the next milennia of evenings she'll sit on that porch swing with Atticus, safe in the knowledge that all the males in her life are unconditionally looking out for her safety and well-being. It's a girl's own story.

A Tree Grows in Brooklyn
1945

Francie Nolan is a dreamer with a crush on her daddy in *A Tree Grows in Brooklyn*, set among the steaming tenements of early-twentieth-century Williamsburg.

The Nolan family's daily struggle for survival threatens to kill the joy of their boisterous family life. The increasingly hardened Katie (Dorothy McGuire) scrubs stairs even though she's pregnant with a third child she can't afford, and Johnny (James Dunn) is a sporadically employed singing waiter who has been drinking his tips.

The two children take after their parents. Francie (Peggy Ann Garner) has one school dress, which she irons faithfully each night, but keeps herself going with fantasies of a beautiful life. Younger brother Neeley (Ted Donaldson) is as practical as his mom; he pulls innocent street scams to raise pennies and knows all the tricks about how to get the best (and cheapest) day-old bread.

The difference between the parents is summed up by their reactions to a sickly little girl who lives downstairs. Katie sees the girl's new dress and guesses it means she's feeling much better; this sends the dying child into tears. Johnny sees the dress and realizes what it means to the girl, and he makes a show of telling her how like a princess she looks. Katie would have saved the dress money for a proper funeral, while Johnny would have gone for the dress or whatever it took to give the child a few happy moments while alive.

Johnny is one of those happy-go-lucky drunks who fills his daughter's head with promises of the riches they will have when his "ship comes in." Only as she gets older and begins to have real goals does Francie understand that the ship is never coming in and that daddy's pipe dreams carry the cost of a disappointment on the horizon.

Rather than let her down, Johnny does one great thing for Francie

Peggy Ann Garner's unshakable faith in her alcoholic father is the cornerstone of *A Tree Grows in Brooklyn*. From left: Lloyd Nolan, Joan Blondell, parents Dorothy McGuire and James Dunn, and kids Ted Donaldson and Peggy Ann Garner.

before he dies on the streets of pneumonia. He lies for her to help her get into a better-zoned school, where she'll have a chance to realize her potential. It is at this school, with a kind teacher and friendly classmates, that Francie decides to become a writer, a way in which she can still flesh out her dreams without necessarily buying into them.

The tree that forces itself through the cement cracks of the courtyard is the metaphor for Francie's and other immigrants' descendants' ability to blossom in an inhospitable environment.

This was McGuire's second film role, and she got it only after Gene Tierney became pregnant. Peggy Ann Garner won a special child actress Oscar for her performance. And James Dunn, a drinker himself, rewarded Darryl Zanuck's faith in him by winning a Best Supporting

Actor Oscar for playing the harmless Irish tippler who disappoints his family one too many times, yet leaves a legacy all his own that has nothing to do with money. "Bend down, Papa," Francie says to her dad after he gets her into the high school that will make all the difference in her life. He puts his ear next to her lips. "My cup runneth over."

In addition to having some of the most emotionally natural father-daughter scenes of any movie, *A Tree Grows in Brooklyn* also portrays mother-daughter tensions that arise when daughter holds the catbird's seat of Daddy's Little Girl. After Johnny's death, Francie resents her mom for having been so hard on him but is torn by her mother's special need for her when it's time to have the baby.

There are also some great scenes filmed by first-time film director Elia Kazan between McGuire and Joan Blondell as the good-time sister who goes after men as tenaciously as the roots springing from that tree.

Francie learns in one movie what it takes most girls a lifetime—to appreciate both parents and forgive them their faults.

HURTS SO GOOD

Women are very sensitive to charges of masochistic longing.
But let's face it. After growing up under pressure to be
dainty and submissive, serve as caretaker for others, put our
own needs on the back burner, and take on massive
responsibility without getting full credit or fair wages, it's not
surprising that women feel a twinge of recognition from
masochistic behavior on-screen. Dorothy Dandridge and
Isabelle Adjani want the men they can't have in, respectively,
Carmen Jones and *The Story of Adèle H. Seven Brides for Seven
Brothers* makes those secret rape fantasies palatable. Kim
Basinger finds out just how far she'll go for a man in *9 1/2
Weeks*. And a little spanking goes a long way with Kathryn
Grayson in *Kiss Me Kate*.

Dorothy Dandridge has a way with men, but she pushes Harry Belafonte just a little too far in *Carmen Jones*. Dat's de end of him, de end of her.

Carmen Jones
1954

Under the safe guise of enjoying Carmen Jones as a self-determined woman — "Carmen ain't fer sale!" — female audiences can enjoy what *Carmen Jones* is really about: the ennoblement of masochistic love.

In this all-black 1954 update of the tragic Bizet opera, Carmen Jones (Dorothy Dandridge) is a wartime parachute-factory worker who only wants the men who disdain her. She sashays into the lunchroom and teases every male who hungers for her, but her real target is the only one who doesn't look up from his plate except in idle curiosity — the good soldier Joe (Harry Belafonte). He's enjoying one last furlough with his childhood sweetheart, Cindy Lou (Olga James), before going off to be a flyboy.

"One man treats me like I was mud, and all I got dat man can get!" Carmen sings as she fills her tray.

Her theme is familiar, that old female attraction to the heartbreakers. To that she adds a thrilling note of defiance: She'll take the guy down with her. *"You go for me and I'm taboo, but if you're hard to get I go for you, and if I do, den you are through. Boy, my baby dat's de end of you!"*

Carmen hands her bill to one soldier, who happily pays the cashier, but for Joe she saves the rose she's been carrying. She tosses it meaningfully into his lap. We can't read that to be the flower of her virginity, considering her blatantly carnal nature, but the rose certainly represents her sexual favors. While Cindy Lou looks on, hurt and confused, Joe takes a whiff.

And dat's de end of him.

Technically, the movie is about Joe's downfall. He goes from upstanding soldier to two-time murderer, all because of his obsession with Carmen. She plays him, it's true, but Joe helps bring it on himself by trying to cage a girl who made it clear from the start that she needed her freedom. "Carmen's one gal no man puts on a leash!" She only turns her attentions to the boastful prizefighter Husky Miller (Joe Adams) when Joe gets suspicious and proprietary.

Yet the female audience is not as interested in Joe's downfall as in Carmen's. She is done in by her own hypnotic power over men. Unlike her friends (Pearl Bailey and a young Diahann Carroll), she's not interested in hanging out with rich guys in return for jewels and clothes. She's in it for love, even if it is of the purely masochistic kind. In fact, she turns her degradation by men into a power over them. We don't know what Carmen's father was like or what other factors in her youth gave her this taste for retribution, but we do know that any man who makes the mistake of ignoring her winds up ruined.

Considering the limitations imposed by the era on the material and cast, *Carmen Jones* is a pretty hot movie. Handsome young Belafonte, though stripped of his natural singing voice (he was dubbed by LeVern Hutcherson, as was Dandridge, by Marilyn Horne), sings a bare-chested number in the prison work camp, glistening with a glycerine sweat. There are scenes of his binding Carmen hand and foot, tossing her over his shoulder, tussling in the dirt with her. She finally seduces him by undoing his belt in order to straighten it; he kisses her, and in the next scene it's morning and his belt and pants are hanging open.

There's no one who wants to see Joe go back to that priss Cindy Lou. "Good girls" in sexy movies are indescribably square. The audience is solidly behind Dandridge, who brings innate goodness and sadness to a character dismissed by Cindy Lou as "what they call at home a hot bundle"—*meoww*!

In fact, the audience is also behind Pearl Bailey, driven wild by the beat of "that rhythm on the drum."

Carmen Jones established Dandridge as what film historian Donald Bogle calls "the definitive tragic mulatto." Bogle reports that producer-director Otto Preminger thought Dandridge too "sleek and sophisticated for the role of a whore," so she dumbed down her appearance and physical movements and sashayed into Preminger's office all tarted out, thus winning the role of Carmen.

Dandridge was the first black performer to be nominated for a leading-actor Oscar. She lost to her royal blondness Grace Kelly in *The Coun-*

try Girl. Five years later, Dandridge was the sexy star of another Holly-wood musical extravaganza, *Porgy and Bess.* If she had been born a few decades later, she would have been a major star, but in the early 1960s there were no roles for tragic mulattoes.

Within a few years of *Porgy and Bess,* Dandridge lost all her savings in a get-rich-quick scheme and died at forty-one of a drug overdose.

Kiss Me Kate

1953

"So taunt me and hurt me, deceive me, desert me, I'm yours till I die! So in love, so in love, so in love with you my love am I!"

Words to live by. Or to be spanked by.

The show must go on in the musical comedy *Kiss Me Kate*, and to ensure that it does, star Lilli Vanessi (Kathryn Grayson) is appealed to through her full-blown masochistic streak. It never fails.

Lilli and Fred Graham (Howard Keel) are a divorced theatrical couple who still secretly carry a torch for each other. It was Fred's eye for the ladies and Lilli's longing for stability that tore them apart, and it is the same business all over again that reunites them after a tumultuous opening night production of *The Taming of the Shrew*. The onstage play parallels their offstage squabbling, and sexual innuendo (thanks to the saucy Cole Porter lyrics) is the language through which all the characters communicate.

Fred, the director and star of the show, uses his new relationship with the leggy Lois (Ann Miller) to generate the jealousy that fuels Lilli's performance. She only takes the role because she's afraid it will go to the new showgirl.

A little jealousy goes a long way. When Lilli reads the card from a bouquet of flowers that was intended for Lois but wound up in her dressing room instead, Lilli becomes more of a shrew onstage and off than Shakespeare ever envisioned. Act 1 of the play ends with Fred, as Petruchio, delivering a sincere spanking to Lilli's Katherine.

Lilli tries to bolt, but there are gangsters present who need the show to finish in order to collect on a debt. The gangsters keep Lilli onstage through act 2, so that her rendition of the song "I Hate Men" is more

Howard Keel teaches Kathryn Grayson a lesson she
won't forget for several hours in the masochistic musical
comedy *Kiss Me Kate.*

impassioned than usual. She can't sit down because of the spanking, and
Fred is starving her so that she won't get indigestion during her performance. Spanked, starved, forced to stay onstage and to acknowledge her
ex's new lover as well as the truth of all those who preceded her—it's a
masochist's dream.

"*I've oft been told of nuptial bliss,*" sings Fred regretfully as he plays the
playboy Petruchio. "*But what do you do a quarter to two with only a shrew to
kiss?*"

He then goes on in song to describe in ribald detail all the wonderful women he's slept with: *"And Leeza, where are you, Leeza? You gave a new meaning to the leaning tower of Pisa."*

Kiss Me Kate ran for more than a thousand performances on Broadway with Alfred Drake and Patricia Morison. The magnificently bawdy lyrics are bowdlerized for the movie version, so when the gangsters sing "Brush Up Your Shakespeare" to explain how to deal with recalcitrant women, they leave out the couplet: *"If they think your behavior is heinous, kick them right in the* Coriolanus.*"* And when Lilli sings "I Hate Men" from the heart, she neglects this sound advice to her sister sufferers: *"Be wary, oh be wary, he'll tell you he's detained in town on business necessary. His business is the business which he gives his secretary, oh I hate men!"*

But there's still plenty of double entendres to go around. Lois, for example, revels in her sexual conquests in the song "Always True to You (in My Fashion)." *"If a custom-tailored vet asks me out for something wet, when the vet begins to pet I shout hooray!"* And: *"Mr. Harris, plutocrat, wants to give my cheek a pat. If a Harris pat means a Paris hat, okay!"*

Lilli walks out after act 2, but she's back for the finale. Did we doubt it? "I am ashamed that women are so simple," she acquiesces, "to offer war when they should kneel for peace." The shrew is tamed, just as she likes it.

9 1/2 Weeks

1986

You'd have to have read the book (by Elizabeth McNeill) or lived it your-self to get much meaning out of the sadomasochistic relationship in *9 1/2 Weeks*. Suffice it to say that enough women have done one or the other and are able to fill in the movie's gaps of logic.

Even in the healthiest relationship there is the lurking issue for a woman of just how far she'll go to keep her man once she's hooked; take another little piece of my heart, baby.

Kim Basinger is the bottom and Mickey Rourke is the top in this gloss-over of a woman's disintegration under the ineffable weight of an obsessive relationship.

"How did you know I'd respond to you the way I have?" Elizabeth, well into the 9 1/2 weeks of her torment, asks John. The movie gives him some claptrap response about seeing himself in her, but the truth is that he unnerves her right from the start, from the first time he stares frankly at her in Chinatown to the next time she runs into him at an outdoor fair. He exerts power over her initially and never lets up, and if somehow you missed that quality to their relationship, director Adrian Lyne does a close-up on the POWER button of John's stereo. It's Elizabeth's story, but the filmmakers only seem to know what's in it for the guy.

It would have been nice to have more information about what was in it for Elizabeth, as beautiful and desirable a woman as Kim Basinger can make her. Was it so very freeing to do a striptease for her man? Was she a secret adrenaline junky who had never been pushed to the edge before?

Even without character development, female audiences are more apt to understand Elizabeth than the male audiences who came for the ice-cube-on-the-nipple scenes. Women usually have some kind of flirtation with masochistic entanglements while they're young and easy prey, before they've learned the boundaries between socially sanctioned feminine acquiescence and self-determination. Give men an inch, and before you know it, you're picking up dollar bills with your teeth while on your hands and knees.

That's one of the scenes that was both toned down and then cut from the original version of the movie, which is why it was ultimately difficult to understand why Elizabeth would take the abuse John heaped on her.

Insecure Kim Basinger clings to sadistic boyfriend Mickey Rourke, but only for *9 1/2 Weeks*—just long enough to find out how far she'd go to keep a man.

He has her dress like a man, endure a threesome with a prostitute, shoplift a necklace—all in addition to observing various sexual and social rituals. She isn't allowed to visit him at the office or interfere in his life. She can't riffle through his closets or she gets a spanking.

Even when she's good, she gets a spanking.

In return, he "takes care of her," which amounts to a gradual infantilizing. "I'll feed you, I'll dress you in the morning, I'll undress you at night . . . I'll take care of you," he whispers, mesmerizing her.

Those are words that, if not taken too literally, are what many women want to hear. But John means them quite literally. He spoon-feeds Elizabeth, lays out her clothes, and makes her completely passive except when it comes to fulfilling his sexual fantasies. He frightens or taunts her into submission. At the start of the movie, she has plenty of messages on her answering machine. As the 9 1/2 weeks tick by, she has decreasing contact with the outside world. Even at her art-gallery job, she can't concentrate, because all that she is now belongs to John.

In the book on which the movie is based, Elizabeth is only able to leave once she realizes that she would die for this man on his say-so. The movie doesn't really give her a reason to leave except maybe that she's fed up with the whips and chains or that the running time is nearing an end. This cheats the female audience of what it really wants—to explore (vicariously) just how far is too far.

"Crawl! Crawl! Get on all fours and crawl!" John berates Elizabeth. The audience laughs at the impudence, the sheer ridiculousness. Yet, metaphorically speaking, plenty of women have crawled—and worse—for less.

Seven Brides for Seven Brothers
1954

Just think what they could get away with back in 1954. In *Seven Brides for Seven Brothers*, the kidnap and rape of half a townful of women is the subject for sport in musical-comedy style.

Filmmakers wouldn't touch such a subject with a ten-foot lasso today. But the movie's romantic appeal gave rise to a silly TV series aimed at teenyboppers in 1970 *(Here Come the Brides)*, and it is still beloved today as a sugarcoated rape fantasy.

Strapping Howard Keel is the eldest of seven backwoods brothers trying to tame the Oregon Territory in 1850. Keel rides into town to trade for the kind of staples needed by a ranchful of ornery young men—a plow, twenty-five pounds of chewing tobacco, and a wife who can clean up the pigsty he calls home.

"Bless your beautiful hide, prepare to bend your knee," sings Keel lustily, *"And take that vow cause I'm a-tellin' ya now, you're the gal for me!"*

Keel picks out Milly (Jane Powell) for her sturdy back, frontier spirit, mighty fine stew, and cornflower-blue eyes. She accepts this sudden proposal of marriage because she's doing drudge work at the local tavern and dreams of a house and man of her own. (And bless Howard Keel's beautiful hide!)

Twelve miles from town, on a rickety horse-drawn wagon, the new bride sees what she's up against—a septet of brawling, smelly, ill-kempt, uncouth cavemen whose idea of courting a gal is to offer her a chaw of tobaccy.

"You don't want a wife, Adam, you want a hired girl!" she cries.

At first, Milly refuses to share the marital bed. But beneath his gruff exterior, Adam is a good man with a good heart.

Seven Brides owes a lot to the seven dwarfs. Milly gets right to work

Someday my prince will come, or maybe my abductor. Six of the seven brides for seven brothers aren't as anxious about being kidnaped by the strapping young siblings as they may seem.

cleaning up the bachelor pad, then sets about teaching the bashful, dopey, grumpy boys some table manners. Before long, she's got them tame, clean, respectful, and ready to ride into town for wives of their own.

With ten men for every woman, the pickings are slim. The boys get their hearts set on the best virgins in town. Under Stanley Donen's direction and Michael Kidd's athletic choreography, the country boys compete with the townies by dancing ever more furiously and daringly; the girls are dazzled.

Meanwhile, back at the ranch, there's no work getting done because the brothers are all lovesick and moping. Adam offers a plan: to kidnap the girls and force them to yield, just like the Romans did to the Sabine women. A musical number ensues.

"Them women were sobbin', sobbin', sobbin' fit to be tied," sings Keel, as if quoting Plutarch. *"Every muscle was throbbin' from that riotous ride. . .They acted angry and annoyed, but secretly they was overjoyed."*

This plan sets the brother's muscles throbbin', all right. They ride into town, kidnap the girls, and get them out to the country before a convenient avalanche of snow blocks the access path. No one will be able to save the girls till the spring thaw.

Seven Brides is as safe and neutral a rape fantasy as you can get. The brothers, once cleaned up and shorn of their beards, prove as sweet and docile as those dwarfs. Although the winter finds the men relegated to the barn and the women to the house, the two sexes manage to flirt through the windows. The women are especially eager for spring, when they get to commingle and truly fall in love.

One of the problems with women's private rape fantasies is that they are so easily misunderstood. Men enjoy the odious interpretation that women "may as well relax and enjoy it," as if rape were a pleasurable act of sex instead of a vicious and highly personal assault. Women, who are subject to slanderous labels like "slut," enjoy the psychological aspect of the rape fantasy that relieves them of any sense of blame and responsibility.

A gentle rape fantasy like *Seven Brides* doesn't involve any real rape at all. The couples are already interested in each other before the kidnap, and the women enjoy the sequestered months alone with the men as an artificially prolonged (and sex-free) courtship, a time to get comfortable with each other.

When the townsfolk come roaring through the pass the following spring to collect their women, they find them screaming and pummeling the men, just as expected. What they don't realize is that the girls don't want to go back home. They relaxed and enjoyed it, after all.

The Story of Adèle H
1975

"Tell me there is hope that you'll love me again!" is Adèle's heartbreaking refrain in *The Story of Adèle H*, the François Truffaut movie that understands the complications of obsessive love.

Based on the real journals of Adèle Hugo, daughter of French novelist Victor Hugo, Truffaut's movie manages to glide across the bumpy terrain of the heart. Any woman who has ever pined for a man who turned tail will shudder in recognition as Adèle (Oscar-nominated Isabelle Adjani) tries everything under the Nova Scotia sun to win back Lt. Albert Pinson (Bruce Robinson).

"He has often reproached me for my violence," writes Adèle in her increasingly feverish diaries. "I shall win him over by my gentleness."

Within moments of that decision, Pinson visits Adèle in the rooming house from which she's been sending protestations of her love. He is there to say he doesn't love her and won't marry her even though she has followed his regiment from France. Knowing Pinson is waiting sends Adèle into a frenzy of trying to decide what to wear; she almost misses him while she goes through her wardrobe looking for the perfect thing.

"Please just let me love you!" she begs him. When there is no response, she forgets all about gentleness. "I'll ruin you!" she screams, unable to control her mood swings. ("Miss Hugo is a highly strung young lady" is the way the lieutenant delicately puts it.)

The movie begins in 1863, long before Prozac. Adèle, unable to control her obsessive-compulsive behaviors, becomes increasingly detached from the real world as she plots her fantasy wedding to the lieutenant. She stalks him, spies on him making love to another woman, accosts him. She warns his future father-in-law about him, gets a false marriage notice published, and writes to her famous father to tell him her happy tidings.

Isabelle Adjani is so far gone over Bruce Robinson that by the end of *The Story of Adèle H*, she doesn't even recognize that obscure object of desire.

She promises that Pinson can cheat on her once married. She buys him a prostitute. "Love is my religion!" Adèle proclaims.

Love has nothing to do with it. The proof comes near the end of the movie. Pinson is already married and has been stationed in Barbados. Adèle follows him there and wanders the streets, her clothes in tatters, her eyes vacant. When she passes the object of her burning love, she doesn't recognize him, proving that obsession is its own reward, its own object, a fractal seashell forever turning in on itself.

"That a girl shall walk over the sea into the new world to join her lover . . . this, I shall accomplish," the real Adèle wrote in her diary. She got her wish. Once she was returned to her father, she was put in an institution, where she lived to a ripe old age, writing her journals in code.

The Story of Adèle H is a chilling movie for women. You don't have to be a stalker to recognize the romantic obsessing toward which girls are encouraged. Movies, books and songs like "Stand By Your Man" make a virtue of a woman's indelible love for the man that got (or wants to get) away — the dead husband, the French lieutenant, the "love of one's life."

Adèle can't help lovin' dat man. Her reward is madness.

LESBIAN INCLINATIONS

There are those who believe that most young women go through a "phase" in their lives in which they experience lesbian feelings, but the truth is that women have crushes on women throughout their lives. (Men have crushes on men, too, but they're less likely to admit it.) Mercedes McCambridge doesn't know whether to kiss Joan Crawford or shoot her in *Johnny Guitar*. Catherine Deneuve doesn't know whether to kiss Susan Sarandon or bite her neck in *The Hunger*. Judith Anderson has a morbid fascination with her dead mistress's undies in *Rebecca*. Shirley MacLaine goes wild when she hears that Audrey Hepburn is getting married in *The Children's Hour*. And two high school chums cement their friendship in *Heavenly Creatures* with sex and murder.

The extremely cozy relationship between Shirley MacLaine (*left*) and Audrey Hepburn comes under painful scrutiny in *The Children's Hour*.

The Children's Hour
1961

The love that dare not speak its name did not, in fact, speak its name in *The Children's Hour,* in which Shirley MacLaine and Audrey Hepburn are headmistresses accused by a child of having an "unnatural friendship." Word was that Hepburn was uncomfortable with the word "lesbian," so the only "l" word that is uttered in the movie is "lover."

Based on the Lillian Hellman play about how a child's malicious lie can ruin lives, *The Children's Hour* features MacLaine and Hepburn as Martha Dobie and Karen Wright, college friends and owners of a small, struggling school for girls in New England. When a vengeful child weaves a tale for her grandmother of presumably unnatural acts, the woman pulls her out of school and sees to it that the neighbors follow suit. Within hours, the school is empty, and the two friends are ruined financially and socially. (It's little *Lost in Space* Veronica Cartwright who eventually fesses up.)

Director William Wyler had already tried to make a movie version of the play in 1936 with Miriam Hopkins and Merle Oberon. The resulting *These Three* was constrained by the censors not to make any mention of its source material. The lesbian overtones are woefully absent.

Wyler tried again in 1961, this time with Hepburn, MacLaine, and more luck. He even got Hopkins to return, this time as MacLaine's self-centered aunt, who utters the infamous lines "Friendship between women, yes. But not this insane devotion. Why, it's unnatural. Just as unnatural as can be."

The movie is about the destructive power of gossip. But there probably isn't a woman alive who hasn't had a friendship of "insane devotion," whether sexual or not, and who is not interested in seeing it depicted on-screen.

Female viewers are thrilled and titillated by the possibilities of *The Children's Hour.* They are not fooled by the smokescreen provided by

James Garner as Karen's eager suitor. When he announces that they have "set the date," Martha turns bitter and jealous, just as any spurned lover would. In subtext-land, these women are clearly an item, which is why Karen has been sidestepping the issue of marriage for two years.

Even in non-subtext-land, lesbianism is on display. "Every word has a new meaning," marvels Karen in the aftermath of their failed attempt to clear their names. By the end of the movie, Martha comes to realize that the rumors are based in fact, that she is indeed in love with her friend and has been for years. (She's Audrey Hepburn—who can blame her?)

Wyler bowed to pressure to excise a courtroom scene in which the women lose their libel suit when they are found guilty of "sinful sexual knowledge of one another." But before the movie is over, MacLaine's character breaks down and comes to grips with her homosexuality—inasmuch as you could call it coming to grips when the character then turns around and hangs herself. "You're guilty of nothing!" Karen screams at her, but Martha has already felt the taint of truth.

The Children's Hour brought lesbianism out into the open, even if for all the wrong reasons. Early newspaper ads screamed: "What made these women different? Did Nature play an ugly trick and endow them with emotions contrary to those of normal young women?"

Five Academy Award nominations were to no avail. Hepburn was nominated that year, but for the flirtatious Holly Golightly of *Breakfast at Tiffany's.* (She lost to Sophia Loren for *Two Women.*) Lesbians may have been out of the closet, but they weren't yet welcome at the box office.

Heavenly Creatures
. 1994

Teenage boys have been known to cement their friendships by making small slits on their palms and grasping hands in a show of blood brotherhood. In *Heavenly Creatures*, based on a true story of a murder that rocked New Zealand in the 1950s, high schoolers Pauline Parker and Juliet Hulme consecrate their bond with sex and matricide.

This creative, nonjudgmental film by New Zealand director Peter Jackson remarkably depicts the agony and the ecstasy of a particular and well-known type of female friendship—the kind of heated, obsessional entwining that adolescents often form as their first step toward independence. These friendships are marked by an acute sense of privacy and huge phone bills. Fights between such friends are devastating. "Sleepovers" are not bound by any normal sense of time. Parents often feel left out, angry, hurt, and jealous.

Instead of approaching the Parker-Hulme case from a true-crime perspective, Jackson puts the murder of Pauline's mom in the context of such a friendship, which is undoubtedly how the girls must have seen it. It was better (and easier) to kill than to be separated.

Pauline (Melanie Lynskey) is a sullen, overweight misfit. She develops an instant crush on the polished, fanciful Juliet (Kate Winslet), who has just moved from London to sleepy, conservative Christchurch. The cosmopolitan Juliet is unlike the dull conformists who ostracize Pauline. Slightly glamorous and willfully naughty, Juliet sasses her teachers, speaks perfect French, and defies authority. She also gives voice to her imagination, something the community's straitlaced teachers never allow. One subjective message of the movie is that stifling a young girl's spirit can have dire consequences.

Pauline admires Juliet, and Juliet finds a willing audience in Pauline.

Bonding over a feverish delight in Mario Lanza records, Orson Welles movies, and girlish dreams, Pauline and Juliet form one of those clinging, all-consuming friendships that every woman can identify with from girlhood. The two are so close that they concoct their own secret, magical, fully populated fantasy world, which the movie illustrates with wild forays into special effects and plasticine figures. Actual entries from the real Pauline's diary make the friendship that much more believable.

If you lived Down Under during the early 1950's, you'd already be familiar with the Parker-Hulme case, the era's equivalent to the O. J. Simpson trial. In *Cinema of Unease*, actor Sam Neill's autobiographical documentary about growing up in New Zealand, he mentions living down the road from the Hulme house, a specter that had a humorously lugubrious effect on him.

The girls' unsettling, homoerotic liaison led to their parents' attempt to separate them, an act that seemed so violent and psychologically untenable to the girls that they hatched a scheme to lure Pauline's mother out for a nature walk and then beat her to death. Such was their hold on reality that they assumed that the motherless Pauline would then be allowed to live with Juliet's family.

The girls were found guilty of murder and, as part of their sentence, were ordered never to contact each other again. The real Juliet is now a successful mystery writer living in Scotland under the pseudonym Anne Perry. Her identity only came to light after the release of *Heavenly Creatures*. Pauline is thought to live a quiet life in Auckland.

With a surprising amount of humor, this oddly buoyant movie is able to suggest an array of contributing social and psychological factors, as if the murder were an inevitable culmination of hundreds of pinpricks of events, emotions, and flights of fancy. There was the too rigid schooling, the problems of being special in an environment that prized mediocrity, the lure of a mythical kingdom with its own moral universe.

Plus, there was the girls' morbid fears of confinement and abandonment that stemmed from their sickly childhoods. "All the best people have bad chests and lung diseases—it's all frightfully romantic!" the crazily exuberant Juliet reassures Pauline as they trade war stories and examine each other's scars.

One assumes that most friends don't end up killing their mothers—"the

Kate Winslet (*left*) and Melanie Lynskey create their own quasi-orgasmic reality complete with Technicolor fantasy world in *Heavenly Creatures*. (Courtesy of Photofest)

happy event," as it is described in Pauline's diary. Yet there are so few movies that depict the ecstasy, ritual, and intense demands of these friendships that it's easy for women to admire Pauline and Juliet. They met the ultimate test of the obsessional friendship: They were loyal to each other beyond reason, becoming "blood sisters" in the most literal way.

The Hunger

1983

One of the most beautiful, haunting pieces of music in the world is *Lakmé* by Delibes. More specifically, the duet *Viens Mallika Sous le Dome Edais*. It is ethereal, enchanting, hypnotic, teasing. Catherine Deneuve plays its theme on the piano for Susan Sarandon over a glass of sherry and explains that it is two women calling to each other.

Oops! Susan has spilled a little sherry on her blouse. She must undress, revealing a most attentive nipple. It is to this segment of *Lakmé* that Deneuve seduces Sarandon so expertly that she never notices she has been bitten and infected by a fate worse than death—immortality.

The Hunger is an aggressively stylish, sensuous movie about vampires, aging, and lesbian impulses. Amid billowing white curtains and vaulted ceilings, stylish creatures of the night Miriam (Deneuve) and John (David Bowie) ply their trade—living for the moment, an eternity of moments, stalking New York's nightclubs to pick up their prey. They are not unlike plenty of Eurotrash haunting the discos, except that Miriam and John kill their pickups and drink their blood.

After an eternity together, John is showing signs of aging. Although Miriam had promised him immortality, he is turning into a wizened old geezer by the minute.

He seeks out Dr. Sarah Roberts (Sarandon). She specializes in trying to reverse rapid aging in lab monkeys, but she thinks John a nut case. After he spends an afternoon—the remainder of his youth—in Sarandon's waiting room, she realizes the old guy is the real article. She tracks him down to the Manhattan town house he shares with Miriam.

Sarah is strangely drawn to Miriam and vice versa. When Miriam senses, after Sarah leaves, that the doctor is in the path of an oncoming truck, she presses Sarah's phone number on a piece of paper to her heart, which works to avert disaster.

The sexual tension between mortal Susan Sarandon (*seated*) and undead vampire Catharine Deneuve is palpable in *The Hunger*.

Later, Sarah can't sleep. Her eyes are wet with tears of empathy. She's restless in bed next to her doctor-boyfriend. Is it the call of the vampire? Or aren't these the classic, early signs of infatuation—poor concentration, palpitating heart, seeing your beloved everywhere you look? (Sarah sees Miriam's face in the medicine-cabinet mirror.)

Sarah returns to the town house. "Are you lonely?" she asks, betraying her interest. "Especially now that your husband's away?" (John is not really away; he's just laid out with the other spindly skeletons in the attic.)

The vampire's seduction is like an elaborate pickup. During small talk, every line of which has a secondary interpretation, Miriam plays the theme from *Lakmé*. Sarah remarks that it sounds like a love song.

"I told you," says Miriam disingenuously. "It's sung by two women."

"It sounds like a love song," Sarah repeats.

"Then it is."

Sarandon's wet-T-shirt scene ensues. They kiss. Miriam sucks Sarah's nipple. Sarandon told filmmakers for the 1995 documentary *The Celluloid Closet* that director Tony Scott wanted her to drink the sherry to show why a presumably straight woman would begin a lesbian affair. Sarandon was insulted. "You don't have to be drunk to want to kiss Catherine Deneuve," she pointed out.

Made in 1983, *The Hunger* could easily be a metaphor for AIDS, as all subsequent vampire movies have been. But it is more comfortably read as a case study of the inexorable pull of sexual identity. "There are two different strains of blood present fighting each other for dominance," Sarah is told of her blood workup; her lesbian affair has made her feverish and changeable.

"I think you should see a doctor," her boyfriend tells her.

"I *am* a doctor," she replies.

"And so am I."

But what he really means is that she should "see" him in the sense of dating him. The lady doc should be seeing men.

Meanwhile, Miriam has recognized Sarah's true nature from the beginning. When she first appears at Sarah's book signing, the doctor looks up; she has heard Miriam calling her before words are exchanged. Later, Miriam is certain of her conquest. "The hunger will bring her back."

Indeed, it does. Life isn't so rewarding for Sarah now that she has tasted a bit of Miriam. "After a while, you'll forget what you were, and you'll begin to love me as I love you, forever and ever," promises Miriam.

Meanwhile, the snippet from *Lakmé* was so successful it has turned up again both in Tony Scott's other work (the Dennis Hopper–Christopher Walken scene in *True Romance*) and in that of his brother, Ridley (*Someone to Watch Over Me*). Unfortunately, the music became so popular that it can also be heard in the background of a TV commercial. A love song diluted.

Johnny Guitar
1954

"You're a strange woman," says Johnny Guitar (Sterling Hayden) to Joan Crawford, a pants-wearing, gun-slinging, no-nonsense saloon keeper in the Old West. "Only to strangers," she snaps.

But she is a strange woman, and *Johnny Guitar* always gets a strange reaction. Played completely straight, this 1954 Nicholas Ray favorite is filled with camp psychology, role reversals, and genre benders. It's a gay camp classic.

Johnny Guitar isn't your ordinary western, unless you're on hallucinogens—which you may think you are on if you see it in its original, electric, three-strip "Trucolor." Everyone's eyes are extremely blue.

Crawford was fifty when she was improbably cast as Vienna, the hard-bitten owner of a gambling joint in the middle of nowheresville, Arizona—soon to become somewheresville when the railroad comes through. The local cattle herders want to run her out on that rail, no one more so than Emma Small (Mercedes McCambridge), a woman with a mean, tight little face and an unholy fascination with Vienna.

At fifty, Crawford was an unlikely draw for the slavering attentions of every man in sight, including Hayden as the eponymous Johnny Guitar and Scott Brady as "the Dancin' Kid." When the two men square off, what would normally end in pistols at noon turns into a more creative showdown.

"Can you dance?" challenges one. "Can you play?" accepts the other. And so one plays, the other dances, and eventually the guitar man wins Vienna's affections.

Vienna's fortunes—"Luck had nothing to do with it," she says, Mae Westish—and isolationism are usually the preserves of the male western hero. But everything here is screwy, including the overheated dialogue.

"How many men have you forgotten?" asks an unstrung Guitar. "As many as women you've remembered," responds Vienna.

The morning after she has sex, Vienna suddenly appears in a frilly white gown and plays piano while waiting for her various admirers to be lynched.

The movie's allegory concerning McCarthyism has been lost over the years as the lesbian subtext has been heightened by modern gay audiences. Crawford and McCambridge look about as butch as can be as they squabble over the Dancin' Kid and entertain an escalating series of catfights. The love-hate thing between the two women erupts into the movie's final, bloody set piece, the only appropriate resolution to all that closeted sexual seething.

Mercedes McCambridge watches with a mixture of forbidden emotions as Joan Crawford nearly gets hanged; she's so obsessed with her in *Johnny Guitar* that she's willing to kill her. (Courtesy of Photofest)

Rebecca

1940

She dreamed she went back to Manderley, and she's not the only one. Women have always been drawn to *Rebecca*, the movie based on the Daphne du Maurier gothic romance. It stars Joan Fontaine as the second Mrs. de Winter, in thrall to the ghost of the first Mrs. de Winter.

Laurence Olivier plays Maxim de Winter, the wealthy widower and owner of Manderley mansion. On the Riviera to forget his drowned first wife, Rebecca, he meets and marries the awkward young Fontaine. Maxim is a much older man, a brooding, mysterious sort with abrupt changes of mood and flashes of anger.

Like all heroes of gothic romances, Maxim's behavior suggests hatred and disdain for the heroine — up until the end, when all is explained and forgiven. No wonder women eat this stuff up. Movies like *Rebecca* put a happy resolution on that age-old problem of loving a man who is mean, aloof, and impenetrable.

Max is the ultimate example in this regard. He turns on his child bride with inexplicable rages. He never notices her clothes or hair, even though he had showered his first wife with furs and gowns, which are still in Rebecca's closet. The new Mrs. de Winter is frightened by her bridegroom and by the hostile staff of Manderley. Everywhere she goes, there is a reminder of the more beautiful, more accomplished Rebecca — the dead woman's monogram is on everything, from handkerchiefs to pillowcases. The shadow of the dead love rival hangs over every waking moment. "You must have made a mistake," trembles the new Mrs. de Winter when a servant calls her on the house phone. "Mrs. de Winter has been dead for a year."

Fontaine's life would be tolerable if only she had a hint that her husband loves her. She even offers to be just his companion and friend,

knowing that he could never love her as he loved Rebecca. "You thought I loved Rebecca? You thought *that*?" thunders the lord and master. "I *hated her!*" Dah-*dum*!

Max de Winter is a textbook example of the love object who is frightening and inscrutable. But there are other themes going on in *Rebecca* that rivet a female audience.

First, there's the daddy fixation. It's not just that Max is so much older than his nervous bride, a scenario that always triggers an Electra-complex warning. The script plays up the age disparity and its psychological implications. The shy Fontaine first comes alive when describing her recently deceased father—how well they got along. Later, frustrated with her own childishness, she wishes aloud that she were thirty-six and dressed in black evening gown and pearls. Olivier makes her promise never to wear black evening gowns and pearls. Then he pointedly makes her promise never to be thirty-six. Apparently, he wants a little girl as strongly as she wants a daddy figure.

He ridicules her when she tries to put her hair up and dress fashionably. And at the end of the movie, his only regret—and this from a murderer!—is that he has made his bride lose her look of childish innocence. All those women who married colder, older men because they reminded them of their colder, older fathers will play *Rebecca* on an endless loop, because the emotional resolution is so sweet and so absent in everyday life.

Then there's the famous lesbian subtext. Mrs. Danvers, the scariest housekeeper in cinema, has a fetish for the dead Rebecca. As played by the piercing-eyed Judith Anderson, with her hair severely drawn back, Mrs. Danvers tends to the dead woman's things—her hairbrush, her transparent negligee, her clothes and lingerie. She recalls brushing Rebecca's hair for twenty minutes at a time. Rebecca even had a pet name for this warhorse—Danny. Clearly, in the subtext they were lovers, and Danny is still carrying the torch.

At the end of the movie, she carries the torch a little too far, setting Manderley ablaze. But before that, there are more than enough clues that

Joan Fontaine made a specialty of vulnerable woman-child roles. In *Rebecca* she walks in the shadow of the first Mrs. DeWinter, whose underwear drawer is still being tended most tenderly by the smitten housekeeper.

Rebecca was bisexual. She used Mrs. Danvers's name as her own when she went to the doctor, even before she married Mr. de Winter—as if she were using the name of a previous husband. Mrs. Danvers says that Rebecca would come home from her trysts with men and laugh about them with her in bed.

At any rate, Fontaine's fright at her marriage and at suddenly being in over her head, in charge of a mansion and expected to act authoritatively when she herself is still a child, is something female audiences can relate to. There is always the shadow of someone more competent, compelling, beautiful, gracious, mature (in a word, mommy). "Stop biting your nails!" cautions Max, as one would chide a little girl. (His proposal consists of "I'm asking you to marry me, you little fool!")

The belittling effect may have been enhanced by the way director Alfred Hitchcock treated his twenty-two-year-old star with disdain offscreen, while favoring Olivier. Fontaine had her own ghosts to deal with—her lifelong competition with older sister Olivia de Havilland plus the knowledge that Olivier had pushed for his wife, Vivien Leigh, to get the role and hadn't wanted to work with Fontaine. She must have felt much like the second Mrs. de Winter, dwarfed by the shadow of other, more preferable women. Producer David O. Selznick had wanted Loretta Young, and Margaret Sullavan and Anne Baxter had also tested for the role.

The negative chemistry worked. *Rebecca* won for picture and cinematography out of eleven Oscar nominations that year and started Hitchcock on his American career.

FEMALE BONDING

There's power in numbers, and when women get together, they can raise their self-esteem, terrify men, or find new meaning in life. In *Passion Fish*, two damaged women help each other recuperate emotionally. In *The Man in the Moon*, two sisters vie for the same boy but never lose each other. A group of stranded old women find comfort in each other in *Strangers in Good Company*. And in *Diabolique* and *Thelma & Louise*, two women are better at murder than one.

A spoonful of poison helps the murder go down. Vera Clouzot (*left*) and Simone Signoret concoct a lethal cocktail for the man they share in the 1955 version of *Diabolique*.

Isabelle Adjani (*left*) and Sharon Stone wait in vain for a body to surface in the 1996 *Diabolique* remake, in which the ladies are closer than ever.

Diabolique

1955, 1996

It is bad form to reveal the ending of the classic Henri-Georges Clouzot film *Diabolique*. But its appeal to women is no secret. That's why they remade it in 1996 (with a different ending!) as a male-bashing manifesto with comedic and lesbian undertones and with glam queens Sharon Stone and Isabelle Adjani.

The four-star 1955 French thriller starts off with Simone Signoret and Vera Clouzot nervously agreeing on their plan to murder Clouzot's husband (Paul Meurisse) during a three-day holiday from the run-down boys' school where they teach and where the husband is headmaster. Despite the incongruity of friendship between wife and mistress, the women have bonded because the man treats them both so monstrously.

Signoret is the man's lover, Nicole, who is shielding her latest black eye with sunglasses as school lets out for the long weekend. The timid wife, Christina (played by the director's own wife in girlish braids), is a good Catholic despite her reluctant resolution to poison and drown her husband. He humiliates her in public, forcing her to chew and swallow food she has no appetite for and putting a strain on her already weak heart with beatings and sexual demands.

The lover is the stronger and more practical of the two. She has mapped out the murder to the last detail, including an elaborate bathtub drowning and the dumping of the body in a hamper into the school's scummy pool. Black-and-white photography makes the pool look particularly uninviting, and Clouzot's camera returns to it again and again as Christina grows obsessed with the prospect of the body's discovery.

As it happens, the body is not discovered. Nor does it bob to the surface or turn up when the pool is drained. The body, which both women have certified as dead, is missing, but there are hints and traces of the man popping up all over the place, including as a ghostly figure in the background of the class photo.

193

Diabolique, like another Clouzot movie, *The Wages of Fear,* is a masterpiece of suspense. Instead of relying on a typical women-in-peril strategy, the movie posits a pair of battered women who coolly take justice into their own hands. The other teachers at the school shake their heads over the idea that the weak points of the love triangle have teamed up, but this union is an empowering one, a secret delight to female audiences whose anxiety over "other woman" scenarios is rarely addressed, let alone quelled, by movies. (Many movies exploit the triangle but don't resolve it to any woman's satisfaction.) There's something touching about the mistress caring for the wife, administering her medication, looking out for her interests. And if all is not as it seems by the end of the movie, at least one of the women gets the last laugh.

The 1996 version, in which the filmmaker's art that made the original so memorable is lost in the shuffle of sexual tableaux and comic relief, is pure Hollywood. "Why don't you swallow for a change?" the husband (Chazz Palminteri) crudely demands of his pale and trembling wife (Adjani) at the dinner table.

Adjani, a gorgeous French actress who uses alabaster-pale face powder like fairy dust, is credible as a woman with a weak heart. When she suffers an attack, her already luminous eyes get very big and round, and Sharon Stone, who has probably had just as many visits to the plastic surgeon, puts her own very concerned, large, round eyes right near Adjani's. These actresses, with their heads together, make a series of very impressive portraits. If they are secretly lovers, as the movie implies, then everyone will be envious, men and women alike. (Stone makes love to Adjani's arm just to check if she's still human.)

The part of the detective is played by a female in the remake. Kathy Bates plays a hard-bitten breast-cancer survivor who cracks jokes about her mastectomy and about what jerks men can be. After witnessing one male's murder, she drags on a cigarette as if it were the best sex she'd ever had.

Everything that was subtle and suspenseful about the original is made paint-by-numbers in the remake, although it is certainly empowering to watch Sharon Stone do her bitchy best. When the detective suggests that maybe the lover killed the husband because she couldn't get him for herself, Stone snorts in derision. "If I couldn't get a man to leave his wife for me, I wouldn't kill him, I'd kill myself."

Passion Fish

1992

A paraplegic former actress and her emotionally wounded nurse bond in the bayou in *Passion Fish*, an unhurried examination of two completely different women and how they affect each other's lives.

Mary McDonnell was nominated for an Oscar for the role of Mary-Alice Culhane, a bitchy soap star whose taxi accident—she was on her way to get her legs waxed—doesn't soften her up a bit. She awakens in the hospital to the bizarre image of herself on the TV, acting as usual in the make-believe world of soap-opera disasters while unable to come to terms with the real-life disaster that has paralyzed her from the waist down.

In her bitterness over being incapacitated, Mary-Alice moves away from her fancy New York life to the ramshackle Louisiana house on the bayou where she grew up. Living like a hermit, she ignores all efforts to help her and proceeds to drink away her misery in front of the TV.

She's so helpless, she needs a full-time caretaker, but the nurses who apply cannot stand her long enough to finish out the week. (The various applicants are quite horrifying themselves.)

Even the agency that sends them doesn't want to deal with Mary-Alice, a true bitch on wheels. They send her one final candidate, Chantelle (Alfre Woodard), a self-contained young black woman who needs the job so badly, she doesn't have the luxury to quit.

Nor will she put up with Mary-Alice's shenanigans. Chantelle is disgusted by her patient's drinking, self-pity, and refusal to develop the upper-body strength she'll need to get around in her wheelchair. At one point, Chantelle simply wheels Mary-Alice out onto the lawn and leaves her there to get back herself. "But it's all uphill!" whines Mary-Alice. "So's life!" Chantelle spits back.

Director John Sayles, who also wrote the Oscar-nominated screenplay, lets the story unfold as leisurely as if he were on bayou time him-

Alfre Woodard (*left*) and Mary McDonnell learn there's life out there on the bayou in *Passion Fish*, in which two damaged women heal each other.

self. He doesn't focus on meaningless action, and he doesn't cheat the viewer or his characters with the kind of quick-save tactics of Hollywood movies—in which Mary-Alice probably would have regained use of her legs and made a big TV comeback.

In fact, when Mary-Alice's New York actress friends visit, they seem so affected and alien to the terrain that, like Chantelle, who winds up waiting on them like a housemaid, we keep hoping they'll leave.

The two women experience the slow and often painful process of friendship and interdependence. They are rewarded with romance, too— Chantelle with a sweet-talking local man and Mary-Alice with Rennie (David Strathairn), a shy childhood friend who is married with children but emotionally available to help Mary-Alice feel like a woman again. She takes being paralyzed below the waist a little too literally when in fact there's life yet in the old girl! Rennie takes the women out on the bayou, a place of mystery and promise. Into their hands he places passion fish, which, when wished upon, are supposed to bring you the man of your dreams.

Passion Fish is about two women who cannot feel—one through the metaphor of her accident, the other because she has been slapped down too many times. They help each other reawaken to a new, more responsible and joyful life.

The Man in the Moon
1991

There are plenty of movies about the noble and volatile institution of fraternity. Marlon Barndo coulda been a contender if not for his brother. But the secret sorority of sisters is rarely explored on-screen, perhaps because it is so shielded from the world of men. *The Man in the Moon* captures the love and jealousies between sisters with stunning, accurate simplicity.

"I wish I could be just like you," complains Dani Trant (Reese Witherspoon), the younger sister, as the two get ready for bed. "I'm just a lump."

Dani is a bright, energetic girl of fourteen right on the cusp of womanhood. She belongs to a big, loving family, with a baby sister and another infant on the way. In the summer, she and older sister Maureen (Emily Warfield) sleep on the screened-in porch and talk late into the night, brushing each other's hair, listening to Elvis Presley records, gazing into the future. During the day, Dani runs off to the local swimming hole whenever she gets the chance, jumping in naked without fear of discovery.

One day, she is discovered. An older boy jumps into the water and turns out to be Court (Jason London), the son of her mother's long-time best friend. The recently widowed friend has just moved back onto the long-deserted property that encompasses the swimming hole.

At first, Dani is resentful of the intrusion. But she softens as the boy pays her attention and becomes a secret playmate. Now Dani is a changed little girl, helping around the house, whistling a happy tune. She hugs and kisses her pillow at night—practicing—and struggles with her new-found electricity. "If I do what I feel," she tells her amused sister, "I'll just burst into pieces and go flying into space!"

Court enjoys Dani's company, but he doesn't mistake her for anything other than what she is. "You're a little girl, and you don't know what you're doing," he tells her when she purses her lips and adopts a kiss-me pose.

The Man in the Moon's Reese Witherspoon leans in for her first kiss, from neighbor Jason London, before the boy takes up with her more age-appropriate older sister. (Courtesy of Photofest)

If that shatters her world, worse is to come. Once Court beholds Dani's seventeen-year-old sister, who is truly ripe for kissing, Dani is left out of the loop. Nature's timeless dance of billing and cooing ensues, with Dani a resentful spectator. To her, it feels as if the sister she loved and trusted has betrayed her to the core. One can imagine this being replayed later in Dani's life, because as all sisters know, those early feelings of admiration and rivalry crop up again and again in a girl's life.

The Man in the Moon paints a constellation of a young girl's world. She is the apple of her father's eye, so that when he gets angry and beats her with a belt one night, the humiliation of it far exceeds any physical pain.

In general, what movies know about sisterhood can be summed up by *What Ever Happened to Baby Jane?* in which one sister holds the other hostage and old resentments never die. But the truth about sisters is far more complex and less kitschy. Even the man in the moon knows that.

Strangers in Good Company
1991

Seven creaky old women and their bus driver come struggling out of the mist into camera range at the beginning of *Strangers in Good Company*, a gentle Canadian movie that patiently shows us beautiful young spirits trapped inside old flesh.

The original title, *The Company of Strangers*, had to be changed after Hollywood appropriated the name for a Nastasha Richardson movie about sadomasochistic sex in Venice. It wouldn't do to confuse the two.

Strangers in Good Company dumps the eight women in an abandoned Quebec farmhouse after their tour bus breaks down. "The detour turned into something completely unexpected," the movie announces. The movie, too, is unexpected, taking a bunch of crotchety, ill-suited women with different medical, spiritual, and vanity needs and turning them into distinct individuals whose imminent death we the viewers mourn.

Making do for a few days on old mattresses and quilts, the ladies gradually get more creative. One fashions a pair of panty hose into a fishing net, another collects a bucket of frogs to cook, still another makes a homemade poultice for the bus driver's sprained ankle. Some who appear useless prove quite resourceful; others who appear hopeless prove otherwise. An eighty-year-old who is ashamed of her thinning hair whips off her wig triumphantly. A woman who seems too mammoth to budge floats around the room as the ladies sing "In the Mood." A nun uses her overall faith to master auto mechanics despite the trials of Job.

The women gradually come to appreciate the wild beauty of the setting and of each other.

Director Cynthia Scott had only made dance documentaries before attempting *Strangers in Good Company*. She cast the women as themselves, using their actual first names and life stories.

Much of the dialogue was improvised, which adds to the movie's candor. When one bookish old lady explains matter-of-factly why she never lived with men—"Well, you know, I'm a lesbian"—another responds quite giddily but readily accepts the information and moves on to bird-watching.

The movie shows how a woman's experiences, relationships, and personality shape her attitudes toward old age and death. For the viewer it offers something more—a contemplative time spent with older women, a category virtually absent from movies. They are shown in all their querulousness and glory.

The best thing director Scott does is to intersperse the movie with real still photos of these old birds as babies themselves, as someone else's precious little girl, as wives and mothers, as shy or whimsical or sexual people. It takes the sting out of old age.

A gaggle of stranded older women learn about themselves, each other, and old age in the gentle female-bonding movie *Strangers in Good Company*. (Courtesy of Photofest)

Thelma & Louise
1991

"I feel awake, wide awake," says Thelma, former housewife turned road warrior in *Thelma & Louise*. "I don't remember ever feeling this awake."

Both Thelma (Geena Davis) and Louise (Susan Sarandon) wake up from their humdrum Arkansas lives when the weekend camping trip they had planned is interrupted by rape, murder, armed robbery, and about 101 moving violations. "We're havin' a snowball effect here," observes Louise wryly as the two steadfastly avoid the hairy male arm of the law.

"A hundred people saw you dancing cheek to cheek all night," Louise yells when her friend suggests they turn themselves in after Louise has killed a creep who was attempting to rape Thelma in the parking lot of a roadhouse. The more innocent and blindly trusting Thelma thinks that they can just tell their side of the story to the cops and go their merry way. "Godammit, we don't live in that kind of world, Thelma!"

"Law is some tricky shit, isn't it?" Thelma later says in wonder.

Thelma & Louise is about two women who are hemmed in on all sides by the unfairness of men and who decide to break free of those restraints together, no matter what it takes. It's a gloriously empowering movie for women.

Thelma is a rabbity housewife afraid to stand up to her lying, cheating, posturing husband. She doesn't even have the guts to tell Darryl she's taking a weekend trip, so she just packs up everything she can think of—including Darryl's gun, which she holds gingerly, as if it's a dead mouse—and leaves a note tacked to the microwave.

Louise is a waitress at a hash house. She has a boyfriend (Michael Madsen) who can be sweet when he's not losing his temper and who pauses before answering whether he loves her. (Contrary to the male audience's objections, there are several sympathetic men in the cast,

201

including Madsen and Harvey Keitel as the cop who doesn't want the FBI to "turn up the noise.")

Neither woman thinks her life is so bad, but that's only because they're not yet awake. The movie begins with a black-and-white vista turning to glorious color, and that's what will soon happen to Thelma and Louise.

"In the future, when a woman's cryin' like that, she isn't having any fun," Louise yells at the man who is in the process of raping Thelma on the hood of a car after a few drinks in a bar. She has saved her pal by pointing Darryl's gun at the man's head, but as they walk away, the rapist continues to taunt them. "Suck my dick!" he yells. Louise pulls the trigger.

"You watch your mouth, buddy!" she says shakily to the dead body.

A series of bad luck and bad judgment further cloud what should have been a relaxing weekend in the mountains. Without any preparation, the women are suddenly outlaws on the lam, something they certainly never expected. "Things have changed; everything has changed."

As the two make their bid for Mexico in Louise's 1966 Thunderbird convertible, they are surrounded on all sides by a male world of spewing, spraying machinery—crop dusters, eighteen-wheelers, a train that drowns out their voices, whirring FBI helicopters. The only time the women are at peace is when they are wending their way through the magnificence of Monument Valley, feeling the wind in their hair.

Ridley Scott's direction stayed true to Callie Khouri's Oscar-winning screenplay. There are scenes you would never expect from a male director that show an affinity for a woman's point of view. A perfect example is when Louise goes into the ladies' room at the bar to fix her hair. As seen from the vantage point of the mirror, the bathroom is packed with women touching up makeup and rearranging clothing, the secret things women do that make men wonder what takes them so long in there. It's such a common activity for women, yet it is almost a shock to see it on-screen.

There's also the scene that made Brad Pitt the pinup boy he is today. He plays J.D., a charming itinerant holdup man who gives Thelma the first orgasm of her life. She is so excited and pleased with herself the next morning, it's almost worth it that J.D. has stolen all the money they have in the world. The tradeoff also goes along with J.D.'s philosophy that "if done properly, armed robbery doesn't have to be an unpleasant experience."

This is the point in the movie where Thelma and Louise cross over

Susan Sarandon (*left*) **and Geena Davis take to the road in the spirited** *Thelma & Louise*, **but the hairy, long arm of male-dominated law reaches out to choke them.**

into each other's territory. Louise breaks down, and the timid Thelma, who never took an initiative in her life, gets them going again. She robs a store with the technique she learned from J.D. At the beginning of their journey, Thelma had held an unlit cigarette to her lips in imitation of her friend and said, "Now I'm Louise." By the end of the movie, they are each a little of the other, and they figure that sharing one fate together is better than going back to the dreary lives they used to have.

In fact, knowing what they know about the male-dominated world waiting to take them back, there is only one real choice, and that involves the famous freeze-frame of the T-bird in midflight over the Grand Canyon. As Thelma says, "Let's keep going."

THE MATERNAL INSTINCT

The mother-daughter relationship is fraught with tensions
and peril but doesn't usually get the press of father-son
problems. The idea that the maternal instinct comes naturally
to all women is put to the test by Diane Keaton in *Baby
Boom*, while the mother of *The Bad Seed* lives to regret her
killer daughter was ever born. Live-in baby-sitter Rebecca
DeMornay worms her way into Annabella Sciorra's home by
stealing the loyalty of her children in *The Hand That Rocks the
Cradle*. Meryl Streep makes *Sophie's Choice* at the expense of
her daughter. And the fact that Sandra Bullock's own mother
doesn't recognize her is what makes her so vulnerable to
losing her entire identity in *The Net*.

Executive Diane Keaton's maternal instincts need a jump start, and they get one when she inherits a toddler in *Baby Boom*.

Baby Boom
1987

In the 1980s, women over thirty were bombarded with terrifying messages about their slim chance of finding husbands, having healthy babies, "having it all." One of the few salvos against the negative propaganda was Diane Keaton, baby in one arm, Sam Shepard on the other, in the yuppie comedy *Baby Boom*.

This is not a feminist movie by any means. Its underlying message is that a woman can't be a true, fulfilled woman until she embraces the old-fashioned virtues—motherhood, taking care of a house, dating a hometown boy, relaxing at the local dance hall. But it also offers an alternative to being a cog in big business.

All told, the movie appeals to women who are afraid to take a chance of throwing away their Filofaxes and living by the seat of their pants. It's also a smug delight for suburbanites who feel threatened by big-town career women.

Keaton plays J. C. Wiatt, a Manhattan account executive known around the office as the Tiger Lady. She wears mannish suits, plays with the big boys, and never breaks stride while barking orders at subordinates. Sex with her live-in boyfriend is perfunctory.

All this changes when a mysterious "inheritance" from dead relatives arrives at the airport. It's a baby girl, and the squirming bundle is thrust into J. C.'s awkward arms. "I can't have a baby because I have a twelve-thirty lunch," she tries to explain.

At the restaurant, she checks the baby along with her coat, assures her lunch companion that she is all business and can be on call twenty-four hours a day, then takes the baby home to a new life of mess, disorder, and unpredictability.

All attempts to schedule this baby into a convenient time slot prove futile, and Keaton's carefully constructed world collapses diaper by diaper. She loses her edge at work; her commitment-phobe boyfriend walks out.

She winds up jobless. Ostracized by her snobby Manhattan circle for toting that inconvenient baby, J. C. moves into a quaint farmhouse in Vermont to try the simple pleasures of country living and immediately finds there is nothing quaint about it. The roof leaks; the boiler's broken. Her take-charge survival skills, developed on the job, do not come into play among people who respond to neighborliness faster than to barked orders.

Luckily, there is something country living offers that city living doesn't—a real man. Sam Shepard, the playwright and sometime actor who enjoyed a sizable flurry of female worship after he appeared in *Days of Heaven*, is local vet Dr. Jeff Cooper. He's handsome, strong, empathic, sexy, and loves kids and animals. What more can a woman ask for?"

Initially, J.C. rejects Dr. Cooper as "Dr. Charm" when he stops on the road to help her with her car. Then she swoons as he takes her in his manly arms and kisses her as though he means it.

But even Dr. Charm can't fulfill J.C.'s needs as a businesswoman. In the movie's pat but rewarding scenario, J.C. markets her homemade baby food as a yuppie delicacy. Here the movie's nasty edge shows: She charges a fortune to the very kind of woman she once was, the kind who looks down on country bumpkins. Because of these women's craving for designer items, Keaton makes millions off them and ends up poised to sell the business on her own terms. She ends up having it all, after all, with money, boyfriend, baby, house, leisure time, etc.

Knowing there is a Sam Shepard waiting out there to fix your car makes traditional motherhood attractive. In real life, Diane Keaton desperately wanted a baby of her own, but long-term boyfriends like Warren Beatty and Al Pacino just weren't ready to donate their sperm. In the second of the *Father of the Bride* series, her character gives birth, even though she has a grown daughter who is also pregnant.

In real life Keaton went on to adopt a baby and create the instant single motherhood that *Baby Boom* promised, without sacrificing her career as an actress and director. Of course, when you have millions of dollars to support the single-mother habit, it's that much easier to embrace the traditional values.

The Bad Seed

1956

Long before Michael Myers hacked up his older sister because it was his nature in the *Halloween* series, there was little Patty McCormack, with her shiny pigtails, perfect curtsy, and deadly tap shoes in *The Bad Seed*.

The 1956 drama, based on the novel by William March and the stage hit by Maxwell Anderson, rails against the newly trendy Freudian psychology of its day by positing a well-bred little girl whose evil nature is a matter of heredity. She's "plain bad from the beginning," a "bad seed," as her mother calls her. The movie seems to have a vested interest in proving nature over nurture, even if it takes several remorseless murders to make the case.

Little girls growing up on this startling movie stood slightly in awe of Oscar-nominated McCormack's murderous, manipulative Rhoda Penmark, an eight-year-old who makes good on her every selfish impulse. To expedite inheriting a pretty paperweight, she sends its aged owner down a flight of stairs headfirst. To retrieve a coveted penmanship award, she hammers her rival classmate with the steel taps of her shoes until he takes a long fall off a short pier during the school picnic. "I thought it was exciting!" she tells her mom (Nancy Kelly, also nominated for an Oscar) of the hubub over the boy's drowning. "Now can I have the peanut butter sandwich?"

When the dim, nasty handyman (Henry Jones) catches on to Rhoda's evil nature—apparently it takes one to know one—he taunts her with the thought of "little blue electric chairs for little boys" and pink ones for girls. "You know the noise the electric chair makes? *Zzzzt!*" he hisses. Rhoda responds by locking him in the cellar with some paper and lit matches. His death is experienced as an off-camera series of cries.

(Because it was made in 1956, all the murders take place off-camera, but they seem as creepy as today's bloodlettings. All we see is Rhoda's

Henry Jones soon learns firsthand just how evil little Patty McCormack can be in *The Bad Seed*. **But she can't help herself; she was born bad.**

tightly drawn mask of perfection as she skips around the living room in her spotless dress, demanding "buckets of hugs" from her obliging parents.)

Next in line for Rhoda's attentions would probably have been Mom; therein lies the Freudian frisson for young viewers with guilty consciences.

The Bad Seed also serves as a guilty pleasure for grown women; it was one of the few movies during the happy-face 1950s to acknowledge the misgivings of motherhood. Children don't have to go so far as to commit murder in order to be perceived by their moms as demon spawn. If the pristine Rhoda enacts every child's secret wish of killing off all who stand in the way of immediate gratification, then the equally proper Christine Penmark enacts every mother's occasional forbidden fantasy of returning to the time when she was the only female around. (Christine practically swoons when she speaks of her own father and reveres him so much that she has to take an excited step back when he finally comes to visit.)

The antipsychology strain is interesting, given the material's clearly Freudian appeal to the audience. The movie tosses out psychiatric evaluations like confetti. The handyman is "a schizophrenic with paranoid overtones!" snaps Monica Breedlove (Evelyn Varden), the psycho-babbling landlady who cuts a ridiculous figure. Monica is an enabler, always complimenting Rhoda on her "old-fashioned" virtues, "not like those kids in analysis who can't decide what they want."

Monica presents Rhoda with a pair of dark glasses, perfect for disguising her murderous gaze. In the scene right after Christine realizes what happened at the picnic, she is wearing those dark glasses herself, still trying to hide from the truth.

As Christine gradually breaks down under the strain of suspecting her child's true nature—and her own role in passing on those genes—she grows disheveled and neurotic, just like the drowned boy's drunken mother (Eileen Heckart, yet another Oscar nominee). At one point, Christine puts her head on the table and starts striking the surface in a series of swipes that look unmistakably like the spanking a good non-Freudian would have delivered much earlier on.

Between the pressure of the Hollywood censors and the prevailing mood of familial bliss, *The Bad Seed* could neither let an eight-year-old get away with her immoral acts (as she does in the book and play), nor could it let her mother kill her off with sleeping pills, evil incarnate though she may be. Instead, a *deus ex machina* ending resolves the dilemma, and director Mervyn LeRoy has the cast come out to take their bows and prove that no harm was done. When this theatrical flourish is finished, Nancy Kelly chases young McCormack to the sofa and finally delivers that old-fashioned spanking for which this movie has been rooting all along.

The Bad Seed hasn't aged as well as one would hope, but it still has a chilling effect. McCormack's performance, which is both mannered, in the style of the day, and icy, as befits her character, takes on a nightmarish tinge, with those ultrablond pigtails and *Village of the Damned* stare. It is a movie that defies its own images of perfection and allows female audiences of all ages to indulge their meanest fantasies.

The Hand That Rocks the Cradle

1992

Movies of the early 1990s found a new spin for an old audience: needling the baby boomers now that they were falling prey to the ravages of time. With their aging parents, late-blooming families, high consumer debt, and two-career marriages, this huge segment of the moviegoing population was ripe for a good scare.

The formula was simple. A movie would establish a typical, feel-good yuppie venue, a situation of taste and acquired wealth, and then send in a tenacious interloper from whom there is no relief. In *Unlawful Entry*, Kurt Russell finds he is ill equipped to protect his gorgeous wife and heavily secured home from Ray Liotta, the cop from hell. In *Pacific Heights*, Matthew Modine has sunk all his money into renovating a Victorian house, but his investment and his wife are threatened by Michael Keaton, the Tenant from Hell.

Those two movies hit men in their sources of pride—their wallets, their wives. *The Hand That Rocks the Cradle* makes a more insidious attack on women, the ones who waited to have their babies and now must face parenthood, middle-age, restless husbands, and their own self-doubts, all while seeking good child care.

Rebecca DeMornay, as the Nanny from Hell, is just a small step away from that traditional nemesis—the younger version of oneself who will lure your husband, win the love of your kids, and ultimately prove a better wife and mother. Who is so vulnerable as a new mother, with her body not ship-shape and her energy below sea level?

DeMornay arrives as Peyton Flanders, a cool blond nanny hired to take the pressure off new mommy Claire Bartel (Annabella Sciorra). Peyton has a hidden agenda of revenge: She has lost her own baby and husband, and she blames it on a sexual-harassment suit Claire started.

But oh, she seems so good with the children! She protects the little

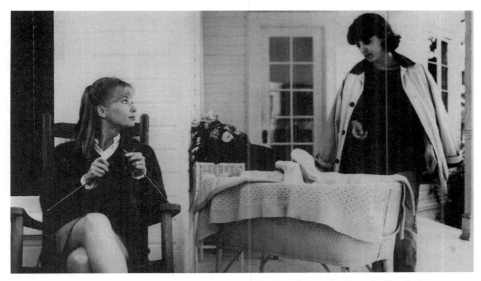

Nanny Rebecca DeMornay (*left*) in a deadly battle with Annabella Sciorra over the affection of the children in *The Hand That Rocks the Cradle.*

girl from school bullies, and when the family is asleep, she breast-feeds the infant so that he will reject his mother's milk in the morning, insult of insults.

Hubby doesn't mind having Peyton around, either—a woman like that with the complexion of angel-food frosting.

The first one to see right through Peyton is Claire's best friend, Marlene (the tart, funny Julianne Moore). Women can see these things from far off. So can fools, which is why the mentally challenged yard worker, Solomon (Ernie Hudson), is also on to Peyton. Solomon has been building a fence in the yard, but yuppie audiences are realizing that there are no fences high or tough enough to keep them all safe.

Will Claire have to wait until Peyton hides her asthma inhaler before she can see as clearly as her name promises?

The movie was a surprise hit—that is, a surprise only to those who didn't realize how deeply the nanny dilemma affects so many women. There's something very unsettling about interviewing young women, practically babies themselves, for the job of caring for one's young and, in many cases, living in one's house.

In real life, a Nanny from Hell can be as simple as someone the kids love just a little too much. If she starts wearing your brand of perfume, look lively. Or at least check those references.

The Net

1995

For the neo-Luddites who think technology is ruining our lives, *The Net* is a confirmation of their fears. The movie anticipates soul-sucking conspiracies lurking behind every chat line. It presents Internet surfers as sad, lonely people who have forgotten how to connect with other humans. Poor, unmarried hacker Angela orders in pizza for dinner and installs a fireplace screen-saver for company.

But for female viewers, *The Net* is about living in the shadow of one's mother and finding a way to regain your identity—again, a subject very close to female hearts.

Bracing new star Sandra Bullock plays Angela Bennett, a computer analyst who can track a computer virus like the microbe hunters of yore.

Angela is brainy, beautiful, sweet, and funny. But she has no personal identity. The proof of this is that her own mother doesn't recognize her. Mom is afflicted with Alzheimer's disease, but that's the movie's rational way of explaining the subtextual problem.

Angela, like many computer hackers, is a control freak. Her schedule and personality are defined by her computer files to such an extent that when bad guys wipe out her files, it is as if Angela no longer exists. Gone are her records, any proof of her existence. She has not made a mark on the world. There are no neighbors who remember her.

And yet, freed from the usual things that tell us what we are—birth certificate, Social Security number, mom's memories—Angela is finally able to breathe. She comes alive only when she finds herself refreshingly out of control. Her struggle to find out who is wiping out her records is her attempt to claim who she is.

The ostensible reason for all this trouble is that Angela has unwittingly logged on to some dangerous stuff. She is in possession of a top-secret floppy disk that could threaten our very government. The computer thugs who dreamed the thing up are trying to get the disk back. Angela, stripped of all identifying documentation, must outwit them, like Rambo in the jungle, armed with only a primitive bow and arrow.

At the end of the movie, Angela is taking care of her sweetly addled mother (which isn't very realistic, considering the demanding nature of Alzheimer's). Mom still doesn't recognize her daughter, but she accepts her. The difference now is that Angela has forged her own personality and no longer needs her mother's approval. While the men are enjoying the chase scenes and Bullock's tight, long-legged jeans, midriff blouse, and fresh-faced vulnerability, the women are enjoying *The Net* for what it really is—getting clear of Mom, the most difficult rite of passage since the birth canal.

Computer expert Sandra Bullock fights back when her identity is stolen in *The Net*. The capper is that at first she is such a nonentity that not even her mother recognizes her.

Sophie's Choice
1982

The choice that Sophie Zawistowska makes in *Sophie's Choice* is which of her two young children to send to the ovens during the war. She cannot make the choice—which mother can?—until the Nazi death-camp commandant threatens to take both children away. "Take my little girl!" Sophie cries, thrusting her daughter at him. "Take my baby!" The son dies, anyway, in the camps, even though Sophie tries to trade sexual favors for his release.

Sophie, played by Meryl Streep with an impeccable Polish accent, cannot live comfortably with the guilt of that choice from her past, even though she has tried to make a new, postwar start in a Brooklyn rooming house. There she is cared for by her emotionally erratic boyfriend, Nathan Landau (Kevin Kline), and adored from one floor down by aspiring writer Stingo (Peter MacNicol), newly arrived from the South. The three become fast friends, but there is an infinite sadness hanging over Sophie.

The movie is based on William Styron's presumably autobiographical novel about traveling north to New York in 1947 in hopes of becoming a writer—which explains why, once again, an interesting woman's story is filtered through the voice and perceptions of a self-interested male narrator. The part where Sophie finally beds the boyish, virginal Stingo and leaves him a note the next morning congratulating him on what a terrific lover he is seems particularly self-serving; women will recognize this for the mercy mission that it is.

Director Alan J. Pakula was nominated for adapting the screenplay from the Styron novel. Of the movie's four other Oscar nominees, only Streep won, for Best Actress.

Sophie's dilemma is not revealed until near the end of this two-and-a-half-hour movie, leaving any halfway sensitive viewer in tears. Until then,

Giving up her daughter is not the only choice Meryl Streep makes in *Sophie's Choice*. She also chooses to stay with manic-depressive Kevin Kline till death do them part.

females are riveted to the movie by a more familiar theme—the woman who stays with a lover whose mood swings prove deadly, out of guilt, gratitude, and compassion.

The movie ultimately explains Nathan's condition as clinically, hopelessly paranoid schizophrenic, exacerbated by occasional drug abuse. He seems more like a garden-variety manic-depressive, one moment leading an imaginary orchestra and proposing ornate, costumed picnics, the next minute talking about death. Later in life, the author Styron experienced a mysterious, protracted bout of depression; one could say that mental illness had been on his mind a long time.

In fact, the movie's title is misleading. Sophie, product of a hateful, vengeful, perfectionist father, and a guilty survivor of the death camps, is addicted to Nathan's on-again, off-again love. That's the choice so many women secretly relate to—linking one's fate to an abusive mate despite all reason, stalling so long on making a choice that one realizes too late that inaction is a choice unto itself.

PERFECT LOVE

Although some of the best-loved Chick Flicks are about missed opportunities and self-sacrifice, women can still get a good cry from a truly happy ending. It's also reassuring to believe that when it comes to coupling up, fate takes a hand and creates a perfect match. Claudette Colbert gets Clark Gable in *It Happened One Night,* both women get the men who are right for them in *Sense and Sensibility*. Annette Bening marries up when she bags *The American President*. Gene Tierney comes back from the dead for everlasting happiness in *Laura*. And Julia Roberts proves—even though it's highly unlikely in real life—that a lowly hooker can convince Richard Gere to settle down, provided she's a *Pretty Woman*.

Annette Bening gets to sleep with the domestic equivalent of royalty in the comedy *The American President,* in which widower Michael Douglas learns how to get an outside line from the Oval Office in order to call girls for dates.

The American President
1995

The urge to date at the top of the food chain is satisfied by *The American President,* in which ordinary citizen Annette Bening gets to share the bed of the leader of the free world.

Michael Douglas plays the handsome widower in the White House who is thinking of dating again. Although his closest friend and adviser tells him that there are simpler ways to procure female companionship for a world leader, Douglas wants the real thing, bouquet of flowers and all.

Bening, a ball-busting lobbyist is currently working on environmental issues, is also available for dating purposes, but she's new in town. What better place to meet available guys than the Oval Office, where there's one in residence whose popularity polls have just gone way up?

The Rob Reiner comedy is a reverse kind of *Roman Holiday,* the movie in which Gregory Peck gets to date royal Audrey Hepburn. In that movie, reality intrudes, and Peck, a lowly journalist, eventually cedes Hepburn back to the throne.

Maybe in Italy. Here the American Dream cannot tolerate such setbacks, so commoner Bening is not only singled out by our equivalent of royalty, but by the end of the movie she is ready for her own anointing.

The two meet when the president overhears the lobbyist maligning his environmental policies. She is embarrassed by the gaffe, but he is delighted and challenged by her spunk. Anyway, he needs a date for the big state dinner coming up. Bening, when asked, proudly agrees to "represent my country," but not before ridiculing the president and hanging up on him because she thinks it's a prank caller. In fact, her reaction is not unlike those winners of radio call-in giveaways who first think it's all a joke and then scream and sputter as if they're won a Nobel Prize.

The charm of dating royalty is not just the specialness of being judged by the company you keep. It's also an opportunity, if not an obsession, to be reassured that bluebloods, like other mortals, put their pants on one leg at a time. Douglas is not only nervous about asking a woman out on a date; he doesn't know how to get an outside line from the Oval Office. He is stymied by the smallest courtship ritual, from buying flowers (how is it done, where is his credit card?) to first-date small talk. Dating is a performance like politicking; he asks Bening how he's doing after the first fifteen minutes or so of their evening.

His precocious daughter fixes his tie and advises him to compliment the new lady on her shoes, but it's Bening who bails him out at the state dinner by addressing the French dignitary in his native tongue to put him at his ease. The two get though their first date step by step, trying to make it look smooth to the outside world while inwardly writhing with insecurity and embarrassment.

Dating the most powerful man in your universe, someone with whom you feel nervous and awed, is a sure tip-off that the Electra complex is kicking in. Once again, it's the daughter hoping to take Mommy's place at the grown-ups' table. That's what lends the comedy to the couple's edgy discussion of whether sex is possible when Bening may always see Douglas as a figurehead instead of a mere mortal.

As Douglas masks his fears by rambling on ostentatiously about taking their time and easing into things, Bening goes into seduction mode. She changes in the bathroom into just a shirt, comes out, and pats the bed to test its springiness. Douglas gulps and endures a tailspin of performance anxiety.

To give the romance a bit of structure, there are allusions to the conflict of interest that it poses for a president to sleep with a paid lobbyist. But *The American President*'s constituency is the legion of women who stand in Annette Bening's high heels, experiencing the thrills and chills of dating the most desirable, famous, powerful man in the country.

It Happened One Night
1934

Clark Gable wants a "real" woman, someone with whom he can hitch-hike, tramp through the woods, sleep in the hay, and have a few laughs. Someone like Claudette Colbert, who puts aside her cloistered-heiress upbringing to do all those things with him in *It Happened One Night*.

A surprise hit in 1934, this romantic comedy set the standard for the ensuing screwball-comedy genre in which two people who clearly belong together have a helluva time coming to that conclusion themselves.

Gable plays a boastful, hard-drinking newspaper man who happens upon the story of a lifetime when he realizes that the woman traveling next to him on a bus to New York is a runaway heiress. In defiance of her father, Colbert is running off to marry a dashing gigolo.

Gable offers to help Colbert get to New York undetected in return for her exclusive story. Though each is driven by selfish motives, by the end of the journey, they are in love with each other, although reluctant to acknowledge it. After several tentative displays of tenderness—he forages for carrots for her; she gets hysterical thinking he has left her—they nearly kiss. Their lips come within inches, and Colbert is shot through a lens covered in Vaseline to enhance her dewy beauty.

It takes several more misunderstandings before Colbert gathers up her wedding dress and runs from the altar in search of the man she truly loves, the "real" man, who values honor (and good times) over money.

Their journey to New York has been a chaste one, thanks to the Wall of Jericho, a blanket strung on a rope between their two single motel beds. The movie's famous ending is a trumpet call and a shot of the blanket falling to the floor.

No one had high hopes for the movie. Clark Gable and Claudette Colbert were both resentful at having to make it. Gable was sent there

Madcap heiress Claudette Colbert is on the run, but not
so fast that reporter Clark Gable can't catch her in
It Happened One Night.

as punishment by M.G.M. for using ill health as an excuse not to do a
picture with Joan Crawford; Colbert only did it for the money (twice
her usual fee) after the role was turned down by Myrna Loy, Margaret
Sullavan, Miriam Hopkins, and Constance Bennett. Colbert squabbled
constantly with director Frank Capra and nearly didn't do the famous
hitchhiking scene in which, after Gable fails to thumb them a ride, she
simply raises her skirt to mid-thigh, causing driver Alan Hale to screech
to a stop. "It's a system all my own," she tells Gable smugly, who gripes,
"Why don't you take off all your clothes and stop forty cars?"

The Depression-era audience ate it up not only for the comedy but
because it extolled the virtues of poverty. Sales of undershirts fell dramatically across the country after audiences saw that sexy Clark Gable
didn't need one in the scene where he begins undressing in front of the

heiress (she runs behind the Wall of Jericho when he reaches for his belt buckle.)

Nevertheless, Gable and Colbert were as surprised as anyone when the movie won all five of the Oscars for which it was nominated, including Best Picture, Director, Actor, and Actress.

The movie is just as appealing today. Although it is Gable who grouses that it's hard to find a "real" woman, the real women in the audience are just as distressed about the possibilities of finding a real man, in 1934 as today. Gable is dashingly virile, coolheaded in emergencies, gentlemanly, forceful (he scares off someone who is on to them by claiming to be a mobster), practical, amusing, and earthy. Once he established this persona in *It Happened One Night,* the public always expected no less (or different) of him.

Siding with Colbert's character is not such a stretch, either, even if she *is* a madcap heiress. You don't have to be rich to identify with a sheltered upbringing, that is filled with restrictions on what "good" girls do. (The bad ones do all the fun things, like hitchhiking, sleeping in the hay, etc., but they lose their reputation in the process.) Leading the vagabond life safely for a couple of days with a brute is a great romantic fantasy, especially if you never have to do it for real.

Laura

1944

"Never has a woman been so beautiful, so exotic, so dangerous to know!" promised the original trailer for the 1944 film noir *Laura*.

Imagine your allure being so great that a man could fall in love with you just by staring at your portrait. The whole of *Laura* is like a teenager's fantasy of dying just so she can see who comes to the funeral and how upset they are. Everyone is in love with Laura, from the maid who found her dead on the floor, to the acerbic columnist ("I write with a goose quill dipped in venom") who took her under his wing, to the detective who has been brought in to solve the murder. ("I suspect everyone and no one!" is one of the movie's enduring legacies, for better or worse.)

Dana Andrews plays the detective who, as columnist Waldo Lydecker (Clifton Webb) points out, is obsessed with the corpse of a woman he never met. He goes through her closet, fingers her lingerie, inhales her perfume, falls asleep in her armchair under the watchful eyes of her portrait.

When he awakens, it is as if to his own dream, for there is Laura, in the flesh. Or at least in Gene Tierney's flesh. Apparently, the wrong girl has been murdered, and Laura was in her country house the whole time. The culprit probably does not know yet that Laura is still alive—unless it was Laura herself who killed the other woman.

"Every woman will feel that when it comes to men, Laura gets by with murder!" hypothesized the movie's trailer. "Every man will feel that when it comes to murder, it couldn't involve a more enticing girl!"

For women, Laura represents such empowerment that it emanates from beyond the grave. Thoughts of her disturb the sleep of the guilty and the innocent. For men, she is—let's face it—a necrophiliac's delight. There has always been something a bit sick about this movie.

While male viewers are falling in love with that portrait themselves,

Dana Andrews is obsessed with a portrait of Gene Tierney and wakes to find that his dream woman isn't dead, after all, in the murder mystery *Laura*.

female viewers are identifying from the sidelines with the supposedly dead woman. Being adored serves some of the same emotional needs as women's secret rape fantasies; it takes matters out of your hands. The adored one is completely passive, neither aware of nor accountable for her admirers' passions. The sleeping beauty in question could be dead or just incommunicado; either way, she is at the heart of the movie without being responsible for the trail of blood and tears.

This yearning to be adored is more than satisfied for Laura. Someone has tried to kill her in a crime of passion, and it could have been one of several ardent admirers, including fiancé Vincent Price or a jealous rival, including Judith Anderson.

The only person we're sure didn't commit the murder is the detective, which makes his obsession with Laura safe. In going through her love letters and fantasizing about her, he is little different from the murderer he seeks. And this is what women want, someone whose pathological adoration is sanctified. It's a detective's job, after all, to snoop around, monitor phone calls, and have your other boyfriends followed and harassed.

The portrait of Laura that gets everyone going is actually a photograph of Gene Tierney, touched up slightly with paint. This was director-producer Otto Preminger's idea, along with trashing the rest of the set design and footage that had been compiled under the short directorial reign of Rouben Mamoulian.

The Waldo character's acerbic personality was supposedly based on Algonquin round-table member Alexander Woolcott. "With you a lean, strong body is the measure of a man," Waldo spits at Laura when he sees she prefers the company of the more virile detective. Early in the film, the detective smirks at Waldo's naked body getting out of the tub; now we know what the cop has that the columnist doesn't.

Clifton Webb was nominated for a supporting Oscar for his Waldo, but of a total of five nominations for the film, only Joseph LaShelle won for cinematography.

Laura runs the risk of proving less interesting alive than she did dead. But she redeems herself—at least for female viewers—when she tells the detective, "I never have been and never will be bound by anything I don't do of my own free will."

She is able to remain just elusive enough that men will continue their slavish devotion to her long after the movie ends.

Pretty Woman

1990

Once again, Richard Gere plays an officer and a gentleman. And a john.

In *Pretty Woman,* Gere reprises the role of the knight in shining armor who will sweep a woman off her feet and take her away from the life of drudgery that almost certainly awaits her.

In *An Officer and a Gentleman,* he literally swept Debra Winger off her feet and carried her out of the factory. In *Pretty Woman,* his white charger is a limousine, and the damsel in distress is Julia Roberts, the most attractive hooker ever to pound the pavement of Hollywood Boulevard.

Gere is Edward Lewis, a corporate takeover artist right out of the take-no-prisoners mid-1980s (although the movie was made in 1990). He's wealthy, handsome, but so unable to take an emotional leap that his girlfriend has already walked out on him as the movie begins.

As this is a rescue fantasy that works two ways, for both men and women, it is only fitting that Edward is "lost" when he first meets Vivian Ward (Roberts) plying her trade. He can't find his way back to Beverly Hills. Vivian can show him the way.

He brings Vivian up to his hotel penthouse for a night. Comedy director Garry Marshall takes the sting out of Vivian's line of work by showing what a good girl she is: She's romantic (she watches *Charade* on TV), she has a childlike innocence (she sings off-key in her bubble bath). She even flosses before sex, and we know that hookers don't kiss.

It's important for the audience to believe that Vivian is a good girl, because prostitution is too tacky a profession for romantic comedy. Few women can identify with Vivian's plight; few men can forgive it. That she is not a flower girl—as was Eliza in *My Fair Lady,* the antecedent of *Pretty Woman*—is because the movie wants to play both sides against the middle. It is a Cinderella fantasy for women, who want Richard Gere to lift them to higher ground, and it is a *Pygmalion* fantasy for men, who want to mold

If you can suspend disbelief long enough—and female audiences often do—prostitute Julia Roberts and client Richard Gere are perfect for each other in *Pretty Woman*.

the perfect woman out of nothing. One of the most cherished male fantasies is that the paid-for whore really does love them above all other johns, really does reach climax, and really does mean all those compliments she whispers throatily in bed.

Edward hires Vivian as his consort for a few days while he cements a business deal. She must learn sophistication practically overnight. Hotel manager Hector Elizondo teaches her table manners. Edward gives her carte blanche on Rodeo Drive. (Here's where the *Pretty Woman* theme song pops up, during a shopping-spree montage.) The rain in Spain stays mainly on the plain; now Vivian is ready to be introduced to society.

The classy john falls in love. Who could resist such a sprite as Vivian, whose earthy honesty is refreshing in Edward's uptight world? Through her, Edward learns to take a chance, to lean over the precipice just a bit. (He's afraid of heights.) Through him Vivian gets polish, clothing, money, security, and the ability to bail out her loyal hooker-roommate (Laura San Giacomo, another "good girl" who sells her body indiscriminately but sleeps with a teddy bear).

The movie hit a nerve with both sexes. It uses fairly-tale logic to manipulate emotions and press the hot buttons. The urge for salvation is a potent one.

Still, there is something dismal about the movie's studiously romantic vision. The original script had a much more appropriately darker ending, and that was the movie Roberts thought she was signing on for. That scenario was changed for the usual commercial reasons.

But just imagine the balance of power in this relationship after the ending credits. Edward has only known Vivian by paying for her professional services. How will each of them feel about the arrangement when Vivian provides the same services for free? Or in a barter arrangement whereby she offers sex and companionship and he offers access to Rodeo Drive? Can he ever forget the dozens of partners before him who received the same services?

How much would you bet that during their first marital squabble he damns her as a whore?

Women want love to conquer all, and *Pretty Woman* fulfills this impossible demand as long as you don't peek beneath the surface. Plenty of women love it, but they may wake up hating themselves the morning after.

Sense and Sensibility

1995

It says a lot about the eternal predictability of love that after filming *Sense and Sensibility*, Emma Thompson dated costar Greg Wise. As usual, the heart rushes in where the mind fears to tread.

What's amusing about this real-life pairing is that in the movie Thompson plays a woman who never stoops to crass emotion, while Wise plays the dashing gigolo on whom foolish girls festoon their maidenheads. If there is anything to be learned about love in *Sense and Sensibility*, it surely wasn't interfering with Emma and Greg's first date.

The movie is about love as we wish it to be, not as it necessarily is.

Two suddenly penniless sisters must find a new window on romantic and financial possibilities in order to get by. Thompson plays Elinor, a thinking creature, while Kate Winslet (of *Heavenly Creatures*) plays Marianne, the sister who is governed by her passions. Neither sister will find true love in the eighteenth-century English countryside until each learns to meld mind and heart, sense and sensibility. Until then, it's a comedy of manners and shallow thinking.

Thompson won an Oscar for adapting Jane Austen's anthropological satire of the mating habits of the English upper classes. The movie followed on the sprightly heels of *Clueless* and *Persuasion*, likewise adaptations of the suddenly popular Austen. Like the writer's other novels, this one deals with the conundrums of being female and marriageable in a controlling social environment.

Fresh from his Hollywood hooker scandal—once again demonstrating the gulf between head and heart—buttoned-down Hugh Grant plays Edward, the shy fumbler from the very family that robbed the sisters of their inheritance. In spite of Edward's genes (and Grant's typically mannered performance, the cinema of nervous tics), Elinor is smitten.

"I greatly esteem him" is her repressed idea of a declaration of love.

There's someone perfect for everyone in *Sense and Sensibility*. Couple number
one: emotional Kate Winslet and brooding Alan Rickman. Couple number two:
sensible Emma Thompson and fumbling Hugh Grant.

Meanwhile, Marianne ignores the romantically brooding Colonel Brandon. (Is she nuts? He's played by Alan Rickman!) Instead, she favors the dashing Willoughby (Greg Wise), who proves that no matter what century you live in, the guy who rides in on the white charger is likely to switch to a Trojan horse in midstream.

"To love is to burn!" Marianne announces breathlessly, then proceeds to get singed.

You'd expect this period to be a Merchant-Ivory epic—but no, it was directed by Ang Lee, whose popular *The Wedding Banquet* and *Eat Drink Man Woman* were likewise comedies of dating, mating, and family interference.

In the end, everyone ends up with the correct partner, which is as it should be, especially in such an old-fashioned romantic treat.

Even more satisfying, if truth be told, are the slightly loose ends—and don't pretend you didn't notice them. Marianne gives up on the soulless Willoughby, but she is never quite the same woman again. The brooding Colonel Brandon gets a Marianne who is forever psychologically damaged by her onetime passion. Willoughby, too, is damaged. He realizes his mistake and watches the wedding from the wild countryside, where he first galloped into Marianne's life. He will always suffer for love of her, which is every wronged woman's dream.

On to Elinor and Edward. These two can look to a simple, penniless life in a country parish. They are, after all, birds of a feather. But who didn't secretly want Elinor to end up with Colonel Brandon, a man whose qualities she sized up at once and who would bring Elinor some much-needed morbid passion?

And yet isn't that perfect love of another kind? Two good enough pairings held forever in balance by the tantalizing fantasies of what could have been?

In real life, of course, Emma Thompson left husband Kenneth Branagh to run off with the rogue of the picture, while Hugh Grant returned to beg mercy of his long-suffering girlfriend, Elizabeth Hurley.

No wonder we love perfect movie romances. In real life, love is just nuts.

Index

Numbers in italics indicate photographs.

About the Author

Jami Bernard is a film critic for the *New York Daily News* and author of *Quentin Tarantino: The Man and His Movies* (Harper-Collins), *First Films: Illustrious, Obscure and Embarrassing Movie Debuts* (Citadel) and *Total Exposure: The Movie Buff's Guide to Hollywood Nude Scenes* (Citadel). She is a member of the National Society of Film Critics and a member and past chair of the New York Film Critics Circle. Her work has appeared in numerous publications, including *Mirabella*, *Self*, and the *Washington Post*, and she has been a guest critic for CNN and the BBC. Previously, she was the chief film critic for the *New York Post*, where she was nominated for a Pulitzer Prize in 1991 for film criticism.

(Photo by Kris Johnson)